S P O T L I G H T

PROVIDENCE

MICHAEL BLANDING & ALEXANDRA HALL

Contents

PROVIDENCE

PROVIDENCE

The story of Providence's renaissance through the past two decades has been well documented in the media and by local boosters, but many people still have little sense of this hilly city of 175,000—the second-largest metropolis in New England. Travelers tend to focus on Rhode Island's coastal half; after all, it is the Ocean State. But Providence has grown into a distinctive and dynamic destination of its own. It's the state's culinary center as well as a hub for visual and performing arts. Providence possesses a larger and better-preserved district of colonial architecture than any other city in the United States. For many travelers, that is reason enough to spend time in Rhode Island, and as a destination, the city's rise in popularity has only just begun.

Beginning in the early 1980s, Providence invested many millions of dollars to reinvent its downtown, uncover and landscape the long-buried river system, and turn itself into a first-rate city. Plenty of U.S. cities have attempted the same sort of comeback in recent years, and few have done a better job than Providence, especially in terms of what the city now offers visitors. Starting with development of a fabulous arts district through sweeping tax incentives for artists and galleries, city hall helped develop a phenomenal restaurant scene by assisting in the financing of such ventures, dismantled a dreary downtown rail system, and uncovered and restored two long-forgotten rivers, transforming a muddled city center into a picturesque walking district that invites visitors to explore.

The downtown presence of major colleges and universities—Brown University, the Rhode

© MICHAEL BLANDING

HIGHLIGHTS

LOOK FOR 🌙 TO FIND RECOMMENDED SIGHTS, ACTIVITIES, DINING, AND LODGING.

🌙 **WaterPlace Park and Riverwalk:** The centerpiece of Providence's dramatic downtown renaissance, this four-acre park and river walk makes for a scenic stroll (page 12).

🌙 **Culinary Arts Museum:** The largest collection of its kind in the world, this museum about all things culinary and food-related resides at the esteemed Johnson and Wales University. Check out the collection of more than 7,500 vintage cookbooks (page 16).

🌙 **Federal Hill:** This bustling neighborhood just west of downtown might be the most dynamic Little Italy in the country, with dozens of first-rate restaurants, cafés, and gourmet food shops (page 17).

🌙 **First Baptist Church In America:** Home to the first-ever Baptist congregation, established by city founder Roger Williams in 1638, this regal building dates to 1775 and is a marvel not only because of its rich history but also its architectural splendor (page 18).

🌙 **John Brown House:** The highlight of Providence's most famous historic thoroughfare, Benefit Street, this three-story Georgian mansion dates to 1786 and abounds with fine colonial furnishings and decorative arts (page 20).

🌙 **RISD Museum of Art:** Much more than your usual college art gallery, the RISD art

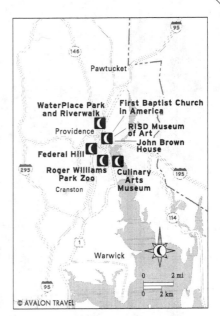

museum is a world-class museum offering an overview of visual art history dating back thousands of years (page 23).

🌙 **Roger Williams Park Zoo:** It's worth venturing a bit off the beaten path to visit Providence's 430-acre oasis, notable for its fine gardens and greenery, first-rate zoo, and museum of natural history (page 28).

Island School of Design (RISD), Providence College, Johnson and Wales—accounts for the many offbeat and inexpensive shops and eateries, hip nightclubs, and stylish-looking 20-somethings slinking about. Densely populated, free-spirited, and progressively tolerant, Providence is one of the more politically liberal cities in the United States, and its most famous institution, Brown University, is one of the more politically liberal schools in the world. Many people think of Boston as left of center, which

by many measures it is, but Providence cultivates a significantly more freewheeling and bohemian arts, music, and political scene. It's less buttoned-down than its neighbor 50 miles to the north, and the high percentage of creative types (RISD is an arts school, and Johnson and Wales is famous for its culinary programs) infuses the city with an edgy, countercultural demeanor that you'd expect more of New York City or San Francisco than of a New England state capital.

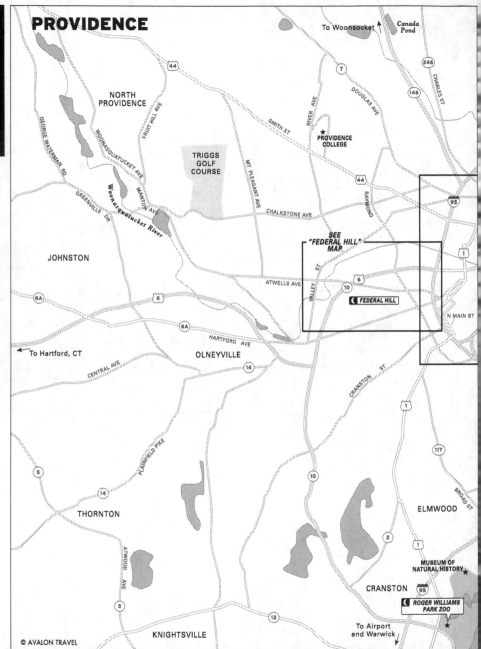

© AVALON TRAVEL

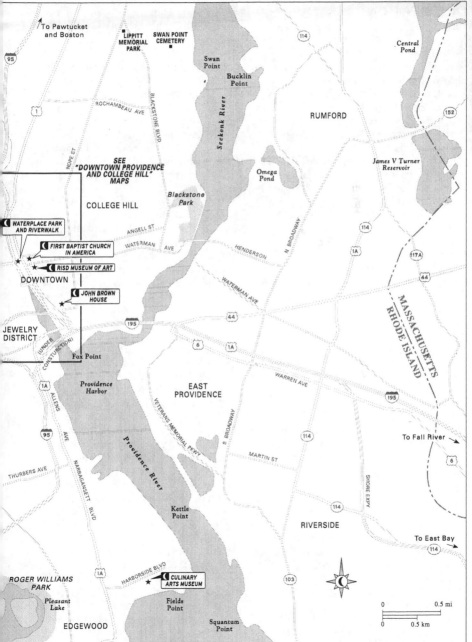

ORIENTATION

Providence is separated into East Side and West Side by the Providence River, which flows through the middle of town. On the east, College Hill rises sharply to form almost a palisade, with Brown University and the Rhode Island School of Design anchoring its slopes. The south boundary of the East Side is Fox Point, a thriving Portuguese community that is also home to many students.

West of the river, a relatively flat network of curving streets forms downtown, also known as Downcity, a business district that also includes the city's major hotels and dining and cultural attractions. South of Downcity, the Jewelry District is a hip neighborhood of dance clubs, restaurants, and stores.

West of downtown, I-95 separates Downcity from the many mostly working-class residential neighborhoods that form the city's West Side. Finally, Olneyville (or just "Olney"), for years the main Hispanic enclave in Providence, has sucked up hipster cred from the Jewelry District and has an ever-changing circus of noise-rock bands, zine publishers, bicycle co-ops, and anarchist fairs among the former mill buildings.

PLANNING YOUR TIME

If you're visiting Rhode Island for the first time, especially if you're seeking a seaside vacation, you should probably think of Providence more as a day trip or at the most a weekend getaway than as the primary focus of your trip. You could see the best of the city's museums in one well-planned day. But if you're a shopper, a foodie, an aficionado of historic preservation, a theatergoer, a gallery hopper, or a live-music fan, you'll easily find plenty here to keep you busy for several days.

HISTORY

The history of Providence is closely linked to the history of Rhode Island. The city's founder, Roger Williams, an early proponent of the separation of church and state, was found guilty of heresy and banished from the colony of Massachusetts in 1636. He sought refuge among the southern Indian tribes, acquiring a written deed in 1638 from the chiefs of the Narragansett people, Canonicus and Miantonomoh.

The residents of Providence took particularly strong exception to financial demands leveled by the English crown on Rhode Island. In 1772 they burned the British tax ship the *Gaspée,* and three years later held their own tea party, modeled on Boston's, on March 2, 1775.

By 1820, Providence's population stood at about 12,000, having doubled since the Revolution—it was the seventh-largest city in the young republic. It remained a commercial powerhouse, in part because of the early industrial successes of the textile mills in Pawtucket. One rather unusual industry, jewelry manufacturing, remains a staple of the city's economy to this day. All kinds of costume jewelry and related products are still produced here. To support the factories, the city increasingly opened its doors to immigrants, mostly of Italian, Portuguese, French-Canadian, and Swedish descent, who formed ethnic enclaves throughout the city.

Providence endured a steady economic decline beginning with the Depression and lasting through World War II and well into the 1970s. The city had nowhere to go but up by the time a plucky and ambitious new mayor named Vincent "Buddy" A. Cianci Jr. took office, spurring a dramatic renaissance that has resulted in the dynamic city we see today. The city reclaimed its waterways by uncovering two rivers that had been paved over a century ago, and Venetian-inspired foot and auto bridges were built over the rivers. The Rhode Island Convention Center opened in 1993, and Providence Place Mall followed in 1999. The city bolstered such successes in the past decade with incentives to lure artists and restaurateurs to revitalize its downtown, a transformation that is still underway today.

ROGER WILLIAMS AND FRIENDS

You don't hear the phrase so much these days, but the greeting "What cheer, netop?" is supposedly what helped convince religious and political dissident Roger Williams to drop anchor at the confluence of the Woonasquatucket and Moshassuck Rivers. The year was 1636, and the place we now know as Providence.

"Netop" can be translated loosely to mean "friend." An amiable Native American spoke the greeting to a no-doubt dejected but determined Williams, who was paddling down the Seekonk River in search of a place to build a new settlement. After spending five years as an assistant minister, first in Salem, then in Plymouth, and then back in Salem, Williams had alienated himself from the Puritans for two reasons: First, he condemned the Puritans' unwillingness to split completely from the Anglican Church of England, a bold step the founders of the Massachusetts Bay and Plymouth Colonies could not bring themselves to take; and second, he believed that the colonies' governing bodies had no business whatsoever monitoring and controlling the religious beliefs and practices of its citizens. Essentially, Williams was an early proponents of the separation of church and state, and also a practitioner of unconditional religious tolerance.

His insistence on articulating these then-radical and seditious views eventually forced the hand of the Massachusetts Bay Colony powers, who convicted him for his contrary and dangerous beliefs in 1636 and made plans to deport him back to England. In February 1636, with arrest imminent, Williams and his wife, Mary, fled the colony, first spending time with the Wampanoag Native Americans between the Plymouth and Providence regions.

After making a brief stab at forming a settlement in East Providence, Williams sailed down the Seekonk River, where he heard the encouraging greeting from a Narragansett Indian, or so the story goes. He continued south and then west around India Point and turned north around Fox Point up the Great Salt (now Providence) River. Here Williams and five compatriots encountered a gurgling fresh spring, where they founded Providence.

© MICHAEL BLANDING

A statue of Roger Williams gazes at the Rhode Island State House.

Sights

THE STATE HOUSE AND RIVERWALK
The State House

A good place to begin a walk around the city is the grounds of Providence's white-marble-domed State House (bounded by Francis, Gaspee, and Smith Sts., 401/222-2357, http://sos.ri.gov/publicinfo/tours, 8:30 A.M.–4:30 P.M. Mon.–Fri., guided tours at 10 and 11 A.M. Mon.–Fri., free). Built in the late 1890s by McKim, Mead, and White, the leviathan work in white Georgia marble dominates grassy and hilly grounds of several acres. The enormous dome ranks among the largest freestanding domes in the world. Free tours of the interior last just under an hour but are not particularly impressive unless you are a big fan of government architecture. The tours do take in a replica of the famous Liberty Bell and one of the famous portraits of George Washington by Rhode Island artist Gilbert Stuart.

(WaterPlace Park and Riverwalk

South of the State House, the imposing facade of Providence Place Mall and the four-acre WaterPlace Park and Riverwalk anchor the city's much-touted renaissance. Once a large tidal basin, the area was filled in 1892 by the Providence and Worcester Railroad and laid over with rail lines and yards. You'd never believe the area's industrial past today: A newly created pond now lies approximately where the northern end of the basin once did, and various entertainment events, mostly rock and pop music, are presented at an adjacent outdoor amphitheater.

One of the more unusual ways to take in the revitalized riverfront is by gondola. Contact **LaGondola** (WaterPlace Park, next to Citizens Plaza, 401/421-8877, www.gondolari.com, 5–11 P.M. Sun.–Thurs., 5 P.M.–midnight Fri.–Sat., $79–159 for 2 people) for a ride aboard one of its Venetian-style gondolas. The 45-minute ride runs the length of the landscaped Riverwalk. You supply the beverages, alcoholic or not, and up to six people, and the gondolier will serenade you with schmaltzy but endearing love songs. It's a good idea to make reservations, especially on weekend evenings. The fare is about $159 for the first two people and $15 for each additional passenger in your group for a private boat. It's still possible to ride without reservations—just show up at the landing by Citizens Plaza, and if the gondola is available, you're free to book a 15–20-minute excursion; the price for this shorter trip is $40 pp. It's customary to tip your gondolier 15–20 percent.

About 10 evenings per year, generally Saturdays May–October, **Waterfire Providence** (401/272-3111, www.waterfire.org) dazzles spectators who come to marvel at the more than 100 bonfires set in cauldrons on pylons along the rivers. The fires, which burn from sunset to midnight, seem to dance

LaGondola brings a taste of Venice to downtown Providence.

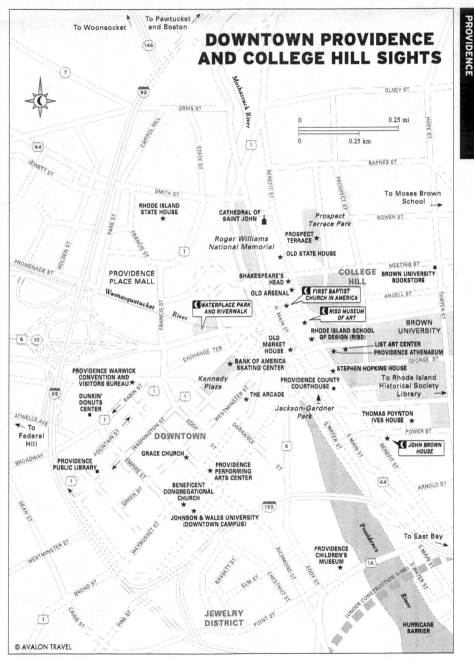

DOWNTOWN PROVIDENCE AND COLLEGE HILL SIGHTS

BUDDY CIANCI AND THE PROVIDENCE RENAISSANCE

As infamous as he is famous, Providence legend Buddy Cianci was one of the longest-serving mayors of a major U.S. city and first Italian American mayor of Providence. He's also one the country's most controversial (and yet popular) political figures, inspiring everything from outrage to fascination – and even a high-profile documentary film about his life, released in 2006.

There's no question that a good deal of the credit for the city's so-called renaissance, as Cianci himself often referred to it, goes to this Huey Long–like mayor, who was convicted in 2002 of one "racketeering conspiracy charge accusing him of masterminding a criminal scheme that took bribes for favors, including tax breaks, jobs, and sweetheart deals on city-owned land," according to the *Providence Journal*. It was the culmination of an investigation into city officials that the FBI called Operation Plunder Dome. Given the conviction, Cianci decided not to run for another term.

Whatever their politics, just about everybody in Providence has a serious opinion on Cianci, the guy *Boston Magazine* described as a "born politician who could schmooze Satan." The colorful, controversial, stocky politico has had his hand – or his strong arm, some might say – in Providence politics since his dark-horse election to the mayor's office in 1974. Given Providence's relative prominence vis-à-vis the rest of the state, Cianci has obtained power and attention that seem more fitting of a state governor than a city leader.

At a time when Providence and virtually every other Northeastern city with working-class roots was down in the dumps, Cianci largely spearheaded an effort to recover downtown from the throes of urban blight and turn the city into a bona fide tourism and business destination. When a lot of people thought the idea was crazy, he believed that Providence could compete with Boston and even New York City for tourism dollars and corporations – and on some level, he succeeded.

Many things have helped Providence to recover, and Cianci is only responsible for some of them, but you really can't help but admire the genius of certain moves, such as offering low-interest city financing to restaurateurs to

above the water's surface, the flames choreographed by artist and creator Barnaby Evans to the sounds of classical and evocative world-beat music. The aroma of burning cedar, oak, and pine lends a distinct ambience to this ritual. Written descriptions of this highly unusual multimedia presentation are inadequate—try to check this one out in person.

DOWNTOWN

The part of Providence that most resembles the downtown of any Northeastern city lies just south of the WaterPlace Park area, bounded on the east by the Providence River, on the west by I-95, and on the south by the remains of the old I-195. Nicknamed **Downcity,** it is less a formal neighborhood than an urban core of commerce and business, though some arts and cultural attractions are included in

the mix. The northern and eastern fringes of the neighborhood have experienced the wave of the city's gentrification, especially the commercial area that borders WaterPlace Park. The area is anchored by the Providence Convention Center, the adjacent Westin Providence hotel, and across the street the Courtyard by Marriott hotel. Next to that, the former train station and nearby buildings now contain restaurants and offices.

Kennedy Plaza

Immediately south of the train station, across from Exchange Place, a grassy park faces **Providence City Hall** and extends across Kennedy Plaza, home to the city's bus terminal, the hub through which virtually every bus in Rhode Island seems to pass. Here too is the **Bank of America Skating Center** (2 Kennedy lure them into the city and out of the wealthier suburbs. In the age of eating out, this trend has helped bring droves of suburbanites and visitors into the city, helping to infuse new blood into once-dowdy areas and to support a slew of related businesses such as hotels, art galleries, and nightclubs.

With the crude enthusiasm and gusto of a used-car salesman, and with plenty of bravado, determination, and innovation, he largely accomplished his aims. But there is a troubling side to this charmingly raffish character. Not only was Cianci convicted of racketeering, he has watched as one city political crony after another has gone down on corruption and bribery charges.

More infamously, in 1984 Cianci himself was convicted of violent crime. It was no white-collar tax dodge or sweetheart deal; he was arrested and pleaded no contest to kidnapping and then beating up his estranged wife's boyfriend with a fire log and burning him with a lighted cigarette. The loveable emperor of Rogue's Island, as the Ocean State is sometimes mockingly called, clearly revealed his unpleasant side.

He spent the term of his five-year suspended sentence as the host of a radio talk show, which drew fantastically high ratings. In 1991 Cianci ran for mayor again and won, this time capturing 97 percent of the vote – astounding when you consider he was a convicted felon and a Republican in a mostly Democratic and liberal state (although on most social issues, Cianci has a thoroughly progressive record). True to form, Cianci apparently went right back to his shady ways.

After his latest conviction in 2002 for racketeering, Cianci was sentenced to five years and four months in prison. He resigned as mayor a few days later and began serving his sentence at Elkton Federal Correctional Institution in Ohio, but of course, that wasn't the end of the story. Released in 2007, Cianci promptly returned to the airwaves with both a radio show and a job as special commentator on WLNE, TV channel 6, where he can be seen every weekday at 4 P.M. in a segment called "Buddy TV." He was later named chief political analyst for the station, disproving F. Scott Fitzgerald's famous maxim that there are "no second acts in American lives."

Plaza, 401/331-5544, ext. 5, www.kennedy-plaza.org/skating-information, 10 A.M.–10 P.M. Mon.–Fri., 11 A.M.–10 P.M. Sat.–Sun., adults $6, children $3), which contains a rink and offers ice skate and roller skate rentals. Kennedy Plaza underwent a major revitalization that saw the bus stands transformed into a new state-of-the-art transportation center. Various efforts have been made to bring the area to life, from farmer's markets to weekend festivals during the warmer months. In truth, however, beyond the skating center there's not a huge amount to see or do here. On the southwest corner of Kennedy Plaza, at Dorrance and Washington Streets, note the grand Providence Biltmore Hotel, built in 1922. A plaque on the facade shows the high-water mark reached during the devastating hurricane of 1938, which ravaged all of southern New England.

Extending south from Kennedy Plaza are a network of mostly one-way streets. The main east–west ones are Washington, Westminster, Weybosset, and Pine, and the main north–south ones are Dorrance, Eddy, Mathewson, and Empire. Visitors should see this neighborhood during the day, not because it's unsafe at night but because there's little to see or do after dark. The neighborhood's main draw is its wealth of fine 19th-century and early-20th-century commercial architecture, although quite a bit of it, especially on the floors above street level, has been vacant for years.

Along Weybosset Street

As you walk south through Downcity, consider strolling on Weybosset Street. Among other things, the street is home to perhaps the most distinguished architectural gem in downtown

Providence, **The Arcade** (65 Weybosset St., 401/598-1199), which dates to 1828 and is the oldest indoor shopping center in the nation. This magnificent example of Greek Revival architecture, designed by James C. Bucklin and Russell Warren, is made of granite and rests under a dramatic glass skylighted roof, its two entrances fronted by a dozen 13-ton Ionic columns. Once home to a variety of stores, the structure was closed in 2008 when its owners began an $8 million renovation; its future remains uncertain.

Farther down Weybosset Street to the southwest is the **Beneficent Congregational Church** (300 Weybosset St., 401/331-9844, www.beneficentchurch.org), an 1809 structure that is the oldest building in this neighborhood. It is notable for its massive gilded dome, which was added in 1836. Only slightly newer but quite famous because of its design by church architect Richard Upjohn, **Grace Church** (175 Mathewson St., 401/331-3225, www.gracechurchprovidence.org, 9 A.M.–1 P.M. daily) is a Gothic Victorian of somber brownstone presided over by an octagonal spire; its chimes resound throughout downtown.

In addition to the architecture in this neighborhood, another attraction is the **Providence Public Library** (150 Empire St., 401/455-8000 or 401/455-8090, www.provlib.org, 1–9 P.M. Mon.–Thurs., 12:30–5:30 P.M. Fri.–Sat., 1–5 P.M. Sun.), which has an art gallery with rotating exhibits.

Just around the corner from the library you'll find the always daring **AS220** art space (115 Empire St., 401/831-9327, www.as220.org, 1–6 P.M. Wed.–Fri., noon–4 P.M. Sat., free), plus the downtown campus of **Johnson and Wales University** (Weybosset and Empire Sts., 401/598-1000, www.jwu.edu). Begun by Gertrude Johnson and Mary Wales as a business-education school in 1914, Johnson and Wales has become a world leader in its technology, hospitality, and culinary arts programs; there are additional campuses in Miami; Charleston, South Carolina; Denver; Norfolk, Virginia; and Gothenburg, Sweden. Television chef Emeril Lagasse, who grew up just over the border in Fall River, Massachusetts, is among the most famous alumni.

◖ Culinary Arts Museum

If you're something of a foodie—or even just like to eat—don't miss the Culinary Arts Museum (315 Harborside Blvd., 401/598-2805, www.culinary.org, 10 A.M.–5 P.M. Tues.–Sun., $7 adults, $2 children) at the Johnson and Wales Harborside campus. The world's largest culinary archive, it contains every imaginable bit of food minutia, including an exhaustive and fascinating cookbook collection, some dating from the 1500s. Exhibits trace different types of food and how, when, and where they became popular over time, and the museum sheds light on the evolution of kitchen gadgetry and equipment and how restaurants have changed through the years. An excellent exhibit traces the history of diners in the United States—a history that has its roots right in Providence. Other exhibits include a re-creation of a classic New England tavern; rare tableware from presidential state dinners; and the Pantheon of Chefs, with display cases devoted to many of the world's kitchen greats, including many items owned by beloved chef Julia Child. Note that the archives are south of the downtown campus, a short drive away on the Providence-Cranston border, but this is one museum that's well worth going out of your way for; just don't come on an empty stomach.

JEWELRY DISTRICT

Fairly quiet during the day, the Jewelry District comes alive at night as a dynamic district of nightclubs and a handful of eateries. What may eventually make this neighborhood even more significant is the tentatively planned multiple-museum complex at Heritage Harbor, which has been postponed indefinitely. The complex was being developed inside a neoclassical turn-of-the-20th-century power plant on the Providence River at Eddy and Point Streets that had been donated to the city by the Narragansett Electric Company. The structure is within walking distance of downtown and the East Side, which is across the river and easily reached via a short bridge.

For the foreseeable future, Heritage Harbor has one attraction that's open, the **Providence Children's Museum** (100 South St., 401/273-5437, www.childrenmuseum.org, 9 A.M.–6 P.M. daily summer, 9 A.M.–6 P.M. other seasons, $5), which moved from Pawtucket in 1997. This engaging hands-on museum offers a range of cool exhibits, including a children's garden that takes visitors through a touch-friendly tour of trees, shrubs, and plants native to Rhode Island; a fun house of mirrors with a walk-through kaleidoscope; a miniature animal hospital sponsored by the Providence Animal Rescue League; and a toddler-oriented area called Littlewoods, in which participants can scamper through simulated caves and climb trees.

Just a short drive south of here via Allens Avenue is one of the city's newest attractions, the *Juliett 484* **Russian Sub Museum** (Collier Point Park, off Allens Ave., 401/823-4200, www.juliett484.org, 10 A.M.–6 P.M.

Sat.–Sun., $8). The museum is an actual former Soviet nuclear cruise-missile submarine, built in 1965, that patrolled the oceans for three decades before starring in the Hollywood thriller *K-19: The Widowmaker* with Harrison Ford and Liam Neeson.

◀ FEDERAL HILL

Go ahead, make those jokes about crime bosses and imagine characters from *The Sopranos* or a Mario Puzo novel sauntering along Atwells Avenue, the main drag of Providence's own Little Italy, Federal Hill. Just keep the jokes quiet, and don't spend a lot of time staring at guys who fit the image of a modern-day mob boss. Maybe there's a mafia presence here these days, maybe there isn't; unquestionably there have been mob-related busts here in the past. What you will find along Atwells Avenue, and also surrounding the charming neighborhood hub **De Pasquale Square,** are terrific restaurants and food shops that seem right out of a Roman streetscape. Years ago, local filmmaker Michael Corrente brought a bit of fame to the

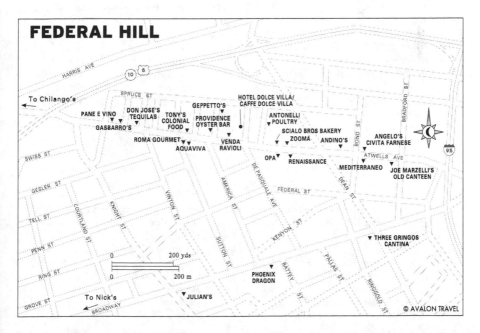

neighborhood by shooting the movie *Federal Hill* here.

The neighborhood begins just west of where Atwells Avenue crosses I-95, and you'll know you've found it the second you pass under the lighted **Federal Hill Arch,** from which an Italian pinecone hangs as a symbol of welcome. For about 15 blocks you'll find shops and eateries offering various delectables, not to mention dry-goods stores and a few random tattoo parlors. This is one stroll on which you probably won't burn any net calories.

ALONG THE RIVERFRONT

The city's East Side is divided from downtown by the Moshassuck River north of about Thomas Street, and then the Providence River south of that. While it is dominated by College Hill, several attractions line the waterfront just across the river. You can get a real sense of modern Providence's humble origins by visiting the site of the original natural springs where Roger Williams established a settlement, now the **Roger Williams National Memorial** (282 N. Main St., 401/521-7266, www.nps.gov/rowi, dawn–dusk daily). This 4.5-acre plot and the visitors center (9 A.M.–4:30 P.M. daily, free) dates from 1730, making it one of the oldest structures in the city; it's easily accessible from downtown hotels and lies just a few blocks east of the State House via Smith Street, at the lower slope of College Hill.

Outside the visitors center in the park, the **Bernon Grove** of trees and plantings commemorates the life of Gabriel Bernon, a French Huguenot who fled persecution in Europe in the 17th century for Providence, where he helped found the Cathedral of St. John (just across the street from the park). Marking what is believed to be the exact spot where the natural springs once flowed, the **Hahn Memorial** is a shapely sculpture named for the first Jewish citizen of Providence to hold elected office.

Just across from the Roger Williams National Memorial stands an elegant example of Georgian ecclesiastical architecture, the Episcopal **Cathedral of St. John** (271 N. Main St., 410/331-4662, www.cathedralofstjohn.

org), which also contains a number of Gothic elements, from tall lancet windows to a Gothic belfry. John Holden Greene designed the church in 1810, but the congregation dates back much earlier, when Gabriel Bernon established King's Chapel here with Nathaniel Brown. The adjoining cemetery contains graves of many of the city's early luminaries.

Those unfortunate enough to be found guilty of serious crimes in colonial Rhode Island were pilloried nearby, at the southwest corner of North Main and Haymarket Streets. The pillory stood until 1837, long after this form of punishment had ended. The home of Roger Williams stood behind what is now 235 North Main Street, nearly overlooking the spring where the state's founder decided to establish the city of Providence in 1636. The site of the city's first mill was at the corner of North Main and Mill Streets, where John Smith founded it in 1646.

The Providence Preservation Society has headquarters at the distinctive three-story wooden building known as **Shakespeare's Head** (21 Meeting St., 401/831-7440, www.ppsri.org). The 1772 house has enjoyed a colorful history, having served originally as the print shop for the city's first newspaper, the *Providence Gazette and Country Journal,* and then as the city's post office. Postmaster John Carter, who had been appointed by U.S. Postmaster-General Benjamin Franklin, not only oversaw the mail; he also sold books and writing materials. A sign depicting the head of William Shakespeare once hung outside the front door to advertise the shop. The Preservation Society tends a delightful restored colonial herb and flower garden (open to the public) behind the house; it has examples of flora commonly grown during the colonial period, including such flowering lovelies as Carolina silverbell, herbaceous peonies, foxglove, and wisteria.

◖ First Baptist Church in America

It may lack the height of the downtown skyscrapers, but the First Baptist Church in

America (75 N. Main St., 401/454-3418, www.fbcia.org) nevertheless effects a more dramatic influence on the city's skyline than any other building. Roger Williams established this parish in 1638, making it the nation's first such congregation. Interestingly, within just a few years, Williams parted ways with the Baptist Church, unable to reconcile his membership of any "earthly church" with his own devout beliefs in the New Testament. In 1700, member Pardon Tillinghast, who built the city's first wharf, constructed a meetinghouse for the congregation—at his own expense—along North Main Street. This structure was succeeded by a larger church in 1726, and in 1775 by the present Baptist church, whose triple-tiered spire rises to 185 feet.

A glimpse inside reveals the remarkable craftsmanship of the times, the five-bay vaulted ceiling rising majestically above rows of wooden pews. Pause to wonder exactly how the builders were able to hoist the church bell, which was cast in London and weighs 2.5 tons, to the belfry. Other notable elements include a massive crystal chandelier built in Ireland and brought over in 1792, and an elaborate E. and G. G. Hook organ that was installed in 1834. If you can time it right, visit during one of the congregation's many wonderful organ concerts.

Around North Main Street

The **Providence Art Club** (11 Thomas St., 401/331-1114, www.providenceartclub.org, noon–4 P.M. Mon.–Fri., 2–4 P.M. Sat.–Sun., or by appointment, free) occupies a pair of late-18th-century houses right around the corner from the First Baptist Church. Here you can visit the free galleries, which present rotating exhibitions of club members' works—this is a popular stop on the monthly Providence Gallery Night.

Thomas Street ranks among the city's most charming, offering historic residential architecture on a steep grade. A couple of doors over from the Providence Art Club, the half-timbered **Fleur-de-Lys Building** (7 Thomas St.) was the home of prominent Rhode Island painter Sidney R. Burleigh until his death in 1929. Edmund R. Willson created the medieval-inspired structure, which has housed artists' studios since Burleigh's death. The **Deacon Edward Taylor House** (9 Thomas St.) dates to 1790 and was the residence of the deacon of the First Congregational Church for many years. The building is noteworthy for its steep-pitched roof.

Just down the hill from Brown University, directly on the Providence River, you'll find the beautifully preserved 1773 **Old Market House** (in Market Sq.), built as the city's agora, where farmers from outlying areas met to sell their goods in town. French soldiers were quartered in the building during the Revolutionary War. The building was designed by Joseph Brown and Stephen Hopkins.

An odd sight along North Main Street, right at Waterman Street, is the mouth of a large road tunnel that runs under College Hill and opens onto Thayer Street. The only way to pass through it is to take a bus across the East Side. The North Main Street entrance to the tunnel marks the spot where Roger Williams traditionally gathered townspeople for meetings and discussions on local government.

College Street marks the transition from North to South Main Street. South Main contains a curious mix of historic residences, funky and increasingly swanky restaurants and a few shops, vintage redbrick commercial structures, and new offices. Structures worth noting as you stroll along include the 1774 **Joseph Brown House** (50 S. Main St.), the home of one of the four famous Brown siblings. Joseph Brown took to architecture and designed this staunch redbrick city home with a widow's walk on the roof; he also designed the First Baptist Church and the Old Market House. Note the **Old Stone Bank** (86 S. Main St.), former home of the Providence Institution for Savings, which was the city's first savings bank and one of the country's oldest. The imposing gilt-domed neoclassical building dates to 1898. The private **Cooke House** (112 S. Main St.) is named for resident Benoni Cooke, grandson of Governor Nicholas Cooke. The Federal mansion dates to the 1820s and is considered one of John Holden Greene's finest residential architectural accomplishments.

Jackson-Gardner Park

Around the Westminster and Pine blocks of South Main Street is Jackson-Gardner Park, a small landscaped patch with benches shaded by tall oak trees and the inspiring 75-foot-tall World War Monument. The park is named for F. Ellis Jackson, who in 1933 built the **Providence County Courthouse** (30 S. Main St.) across the way, and Henry B. Gardner, a naval officer of note in World War II. The formidable eight-story neoclassical structure, built of red brick and limestone, covers a full city block. A four-stage square tower crowned by a cupola stands sentry over the vast structure, notable for its stepped, flanking gabled wings. Few buildings on the East Side command more respect, both architecturally and practically speaking, than the courthouse.

COLLEGE HILL

Rising precipitously to the east just past the river is College Hill, home to both Brown University and the Rhode Island School of Design and the heart of Providence's dynamic profusion of colonial and 19th-century architecture.

The city's "Mile of History," Benefit Street, runs parallel to North and South Main Streets just a block east but in most places many feet higher in elevation. During Providence's heyday as a colonial shipping center, and then throughout the 19th century's industrial periods, wealthy city residents built their homes along or just off Benefit Street, which remained fashionable well into the early 20th century. After World War II, however, and coinciding with the so-called "white flight" to the suburbs that affected most large U.S. cities, many of the old homes along Benefit Street were boarded up, and others were subdivided into boarding houses and cheap apartments. During the city's renaissance, which began in earnest in the late 1970s, the Providence Preservation Society began to restore Benefit Street house by house.

Walking through the neighborhood today, it's hard to believe that it was ever blighted—all told, you'll find about 200 buildings that date to the 18th and 19th centuries along Benefit Street, which is strung with vintage gas lamps and lined by brick sidewalks.

Providence Preservation Society Heritage Tours (21 Meeting St., 401/831-7440, www.ppsri.org), offers both guided and self-guided walking tours of the neighborhood. At certain times during the year, the general public gets a glimpse inside some of these exceptional examples of homes built in the colonial era through Victorian times, and sometimes into the elaborate gardens that surround them. In June, you can attend the **Festival of Historic Houses,** a two-day event of house and garden tours along Benefit Street. Then in December, come for the **Holiday Festival of Historic Homes** (401/831-8587), a Benefit Street ramble that includes carolers and street performers in period garb along with tours of several of the neighborhood's most prominent homes.

One of the first you'll come to as you walk north from Transit or James Streets is the immense **Nightingale-Brown House** (357 Benefit St., 401/863-1177, www.brown.edu/Research/JNBC, 8 A.M.–4 P.M. Mon.–Fri. summer, 8:30 A.M.–5 P.M. Mon.–Fri. other seasons, free). Colonel Joseph Nightingale built the enormous square hip-roofed house in 1792, Brown University founder Nicholas Brown bought the house in 1814, and his son John Carter Brown amassed an unrivaled collection of artifacts and documents here that traced the New World's early history. (This collection is now housed at the library at Brown University that bears his name.) The house remained in the Brown family into the 1980s and is now, appropriately enough, part of Brown University.

John Brown House

Arguably the most imposing of the neighborhood's many impressive homes is the Rhode Island Historical Society's John Brown House (52 Power St., 401/273-7507, www.rihs.org,

1–4 P.M. Tues.–Fri., 10 A.M.–4 P.M. Sat. Apr.–
Nov., 10 A.M.–4 P.M. Fri.–Sat. Jan.–Mar., $8
adults, $4 children). The sixth U.S. president,
John Quincy Adams, described this as "the
most magnificent and elegant private mansion I have seen on this continent." Exquisitely
restored and furnished top to bottom, it still
looks swanky today—few American house-
museums from this period rival it. Inside you'll
find a first-rate assemblage of colonial furnishings and decorative arts.

John Brown, a fabulously successful mer-
chant and one of the masterminds of the *Gaspée*
incident, began construction on the three-story
Georgian mansion in 1786. For many decades
during the building's first century, attending
a party at the Brown House was obligatory
for society types and academics. In 1941 the
house was bequeathed to the Rhode Island
Historical Society, which set about reproduc-
ing the interior's original colors and French
wallpaper. Furnishings include many created
by local artisans William Clagget, a clock-
maker, and Goddard-Townsend, a Newport
firm that specialized in high-quality colonial
wood furnishings.

Other Historic Houses

Note the private **Thomas Poynton Ives House**
(66 Power St.), one of the city's most important and impressive colonial mansions. The
Georgian colonial dates to 1811 and is notable
for its finely crafted rail running along the roof-
line and semicircular portico, which was added
in the 1880s. Another noteworthy private home,
the **Edward Carrington House** (66 Williams
St.), demonstrates the shift around the early
1810s from Georgian colonial to Federal architecture (also called the Adam style). The three-
story brick mansion was built in 1811, and the
final story was added shortly after the original
construction. With heavy stone corner quoins
and lovely elliptical fanlights above the front
door, it stayed in the Carrington family well
into the 20th century.

Governor, U.S. senator, and Civil War general Ambrose Burnside may be best-known for
lending his nickname to what we commonly

call sideburns. The Rhode Island native,
who wore a prominent pair of them, lived for
many years at the now-private 1850s redbrick
Victorian at 314 Benefit Street, between Power
and Charlesfield Streets, a dramatic edifice
with wrought ironwork around it.

Undoubtedly the most kindly street intersection you'll ever come upon, the corner of
Benefit and Benevolent Streets is the site of
John Holden Greene's **First Unitarian Church**
(1 Benevolent St., 401/421-7970, www.firstu-
nitarianprov.org), a structure with a tall steeple and magnificent classical revival detailing
known for housing the largest bell ever cast by
Paul Revere's foundry.

A particularly fine example of a mid-18th-
century colonial home, the **Stephen Hopkins
House** (Benefit St. and Hopkins St., 401/421-
0694, www.stephenhopkins.org, 1–4 P.M.
Fri.–Sat. May–Oct., free) was home to noted
colonial governor Stephen Hopkins during his
10 terms at the helm of Rhode Island. Exhibits
and artifacts in the house document his life
and times as a signatory of the Declaration
of Independence and Brown University's first
chancellor. On warm days, be sure to stroll out
back through the museum's exquisite parterre
garden.

Providence Athenaeum

Among the oldest libraries in North America,
the Providence Athenaeum (251 Benefit
St., 401/421-6970, www.providenceath-
enaeum.org, 9 A.M.–7 P.M. Mon.–Thurs.,
9 A.M.–5 P.M. Fri.–Sat., 1–5 P.M. Sun. Sept.–
May, 9 A.M.–7 P.M. Mon.–Thurs., 9 A.M.–5 P.M.
Fri., 9 A.M.–noon Sat. June–Aug., free), dates
to 1753 and contains such rare and fascinating
works as the seven volumes of the original dou-
ble elephant folio edition of John J. Audubon's
Birds of America. Rare works by Robert Burns,
an early-19th-century study of Egypt commissioned by Napoleon titled *Description de
l'Égypte,* and several books from 14th-century
Europe are additional highlights of the Rare
Books Collection.

The Athenaeum was established in 1831
and moved into this majestic Greek Revival

structure in 1838. In the late 1840s Edgar Allan Poe and Sarah Whitman spent many an hour discussing literature and admiring one another's works in the Athenaeum's corridors. In addition to priceless original literary volumes and a comprehensive modern collection that can be viewed by any visitor (and taken out on loan by members), the Athenaeum houses several rare artworks, including *The Hours,* a famous painting by Newport-born miniature painter Edward G. Malbone.

Other Sights Along Benefit Street

A distinct departure from the many fine residences along Benefit Street, the formidable concrete **Old Arsenal** (176 Benefit St.) was designed in 1840 by James Bucklin, the same architect who designed downtown's Arcade and the nearby Providence Athenaeum. Behind the imposing Gothic Revival facade of white stucco with a giant green wooden door that looks like something out of "Jack and the Beanstalk" it housed troops during both the Dorr Rebellion and the Civil War.

Until the construction of the present-day State House near Providence Place Mall, Rhode Island's General Assembly met at the **Old State House** (150 Benefit St., 401/277-2678, www.rihphc.state.ri.us, 8:30 A.M.–4:30 P.M. Mon.–Fri.), the surprisingly humble-looking brick-and-sandstone structure dating to 1762 (its wooden predecessor burned down in 1758). From its first days, it served not only as the political center but also the social and commercial heart of the colony: In a juxtaposition of politics and commerce, the first floor was an open goods market while politicians assembled upstairs to debate and pass laws. On May 4, 1776, the young assembly passed what is considered the first declaration of independence in the United States, the Rhode Island Independence Act. Surprisingly, the state used this humble building as its capitol until 1900, when the current grand building was constructed.

A short distance up Benefit at stands a lavish private home known as the **Sullivan Dorr House** (109 Benefit St.), one of the city's most admired early-19th-century structures. The three-story mansion, built by Sullivan Dorr with fortunes accrued through overseas trade, contains a magnificent Palladian window whose design is loosely modeled on that of the English villa owned by the poet Alexander Pope. Sullivan Dorr's son Thomas's noble aim of universal suffrage inspired the infamous uprising in 1842 now known as the Dorr Rebellion.

In the 1790 colonial house at 88 Benefit Street, now a private home, lived the object of Edgar Allan Poe's affection. She was a young widow named Sarah Helen Whitman, and the poet dedicated the famous works "To Helen" and "Annabel Lee" to her. Poe had corresponded with Whitman, herself a poet, for a few years and finally met her when he came to lecture at the Franklin Lyceum. The two became immediately and seriously smitten with one another, but Whitman objected to Poe's habitual carousing and boozing—ultimately, she broke off their engagement and left him because of his inability to distance himself from the bottle. Shortly thereafter, the penniless and drunken Poe died in Baltimore.

Farther up College Hill at the intersection of Congdon and Bowen Streets is perhaps the most romantic outdoor space in the city, lofty **Prospect Terrace,** a grassy rectangle with a wrought-iron fence that's perched high above downtown and the State Capitol grounds. It's also the burial site of Roger Williams, whose image is carved in granite above his grave. Surrounding the park are more of the neighborhood's comely houses, and it's a relatively short walk southeast to Brown University's commercial strip along Thayer Street, meaning you could walk off your dinner and woo your sweetheart with a few blocks' stroll to the park.

RHODE ISLAND SCHOOL OF DESIGN (RISD)

The campus of the prestigious RISD occupies many of the blocks along Benefit Street from College to Waterman Streets; there are also buildings down the hill along Main Street and up a block on Prospect Street. The school

© MICHAEL BLANDING

opened with a very practical vocational aim: to train students in the ways of textile arts and design as well as in related fields represented in Providence, such as jewelry design and manufacture and machine works and design. Through the years, the school has gained considerable prestige not only for its applied design courses but for training some of the nation's leaders in fine and graphic arts, interior design, costume-making, and the like. An artsy buzz permeates the campus and nearby streets, and no doubt it has helped to influence the similarly alternative tone of neighboring Brown University, which is perhaps the most countercultural of the Ivy League schools.

Keep an eye out for signs marking RISD's Office of Admissions, which occupies a brilliant Italianate edifice called the **Woods-Gerry Mansion** (62 Prospect St., 401/454-6141, 10 A.M.–4 P.M. Mon.–Tues. and Fri.–Sat., 2–5 P.M. Sun., free). The building contains galleries with rotating art exhibits, and in back you can walk through a small sculpture garden.

◖ RISD Museum of Art

Be sure to stop by the RISD Museum of Art

(224 Benefit St., 401/454-6500, www.risd.edu/museum.cfm, 10 A.M.–5 P.M. Tues.–Sun., $10 adults, $3 children). As RISD is a school, the museum here offers a true survey of works from around the world and spanning many centuries. The collection varies widely, with several works by Monet gracing the French impressionist area and an excellent collection of mostly 18th- and 19th-century American artists such as Frank Benson, Thomas Cole, Winslow Homer, and John Singer Sargent. Rotating exhibitions vary considerably but in recent years have included such lofty themes as *Subject to Change: Art and Design in the Twentieth Century* and *The Figure: Contemporary Works from the Collection.* Guided tours (free with admission) are given Friday at 12:15 P.M.

BROWN UNIVERSITY

Few educational institutions can claim a greater degree of recognition, both nationally and internationally, than Brown University, whose stately—if somber—campus dominates the upper slope of the East Side's College Hill.

The seventh college founded in what became the United States, Brown began in 1764 in the East Bay community of Warren with the name Rhode Island College under the guidance of Reverend James Manning. Despite its Baptist leanings, an early edict related to the school's operations was that "into this Liberal and Catholic Institution shall never be admitted any Religious Tests but on the Contrary all the Members Hereof shall forever enjoy full free Absolute and uninterrupted Liberty of Conscience."

In 1770 a permanent location for the college was established on the east side of Providence on eight acres of what is now College Hill. It wasn't until 1804 that Brown University assumed its present name, in appreciation of the enormous $5,000 gift that merchant Nicholas Brown bestowed on it. Brown enjoys a reputation for being a flashy jet-set school of hipsters and dilettantes—depending on your point of view, a welcome relief to the overly tweedy Ivy League rivals Harvard and Yale, or an obnoxious celebration of narcissistic self-expression.

WHO WAS JOSHUA CARBERRY?

Brown University has matriculated a great many prominent students, from famous writers and performers to illustrious business leaders and politicians. Perhaps the most distinguished alumnus and former professor you'll hear mentioned at Brown is Josiah S. Carberry. A vast trove of records exists dating to the late 1920s, noting that Carberry, a professor of psychoceramics (the study of cracked pots), has given important lectures, published valuable scholarly essays, and altogether changed the course of Brown's academic history. He has been listed in the cast of university plays, served as the subject of more than a few newspaper articles (including one by the *New York Times* that described him as "The World's Greatest Traveler" in 1974), and even been awarded the Ig Noble Prize (a playful take on the Nobel Prize) for, according to an article by a Brown University archivist, being a "bold explorer and eclectic seeker of knowledge, for his pioneering work in the field of psychoceramics."

Perhaps the most amazing thing about Jo-

siah "Joshua" Carberry is that no such person actually exists. Indeed, it appears that Carberry was dreamed up as a hoax, some say by an actual professor at Brown, John Spaeth. Carberry's history is traced to a notice on a bulletin board in 1929 that read: "On Thursday evening at 8:15 in Sayles Hall J. S. Carberry will give a lecture on Archaic Greek Architectural Revetments in Connection with Ionian Philology." This minor event gradually snowballed to the point that Carberry became larger than life. He was cited as having a wife, a daughter, and a clumsy research assistant. In 1955 an unnamed person sent a donation of about $100 to Brown with the instructions that it be used to form the Josiah S. Carberry Fund. A stipulation is that every Friday the 13th, change be collected in brown jugs to bolster the fund. So the next time you hear somebody cite the considerable credentials of Joshua Carberry, think fondly of his legend – and consider how soon it is until the next Friday the 13th, your next opportunity to contribute to the Carberry fund.

Inarguably, Brown fosters a deeply liberal and somewhat countercultural collective philosophy, where avant-garde arts and studies of on-the-edge literary and social theories thrive. Since 2000, Brown has been helmed by Ruth Simmons, the first African American to become president of an Ivy League school.

Campus Buildings

On Brown's central hub, the **Main Green,** you can admire the elegant Georgian architecture of the original **University Hall.** But the university's picturesque hilltop campus incorporates nearly every popular civic architectural style of the past two centuries. Colonial and then Greek Revival architecture (note James C. Bucklin's 1835 **Manning Hall** and also the 1840 **Rhode Island Hall**) dominates the style of those buildings created until the late 1880s, when the aesthetic shifted to accommodate the Victorian movement. A new spate

of building during the 1960s and 1970s produced more modern structures such as the **List Art Building,** where you'll find the **David Winton Bell Gallery** (List Art Center, 64 College St., 401/863-2932, www.brown.edu, 11 A.M.–4 P.M. Mon.–Fri., 1–4 P.M. Sat.–Sun., free), showing both contemporary and historic exhibitions.

Another building worth visiting is the **John Hay Library** (Prospect St. and College St., 401/863-2146, http://dl.lib.brown.edu/libweb/about/hay, 9 A.M.–5 P.M. Mon.–Fri., free) which dates to 1910 and serves as the repository for Brown University's rare collections. These include a substantial trove of manuscripts attributed to Abraham Lincoln, the correspondence of early horror writer H. P. Lovecraft, and many items from the life of Napoleon, among other ephemera. History buffs should visit the neoclassical 1904 **John Carter Brown Library** (George St. and Brown

St., 401/863-2725, www.brown.edu/Facilities/ John_Carter_Brown_Library, 8:30 A.M.–5 P.M. Mon.–Fri., 9 A.M.–noon Sat., free), whose collection of artifacts and documents pertaining to the history of the New World from the days of Columbus until the American Revolution is among the world's most important.

Brown's commercial college strip centers on **Thayer Street,** from about Bowen Street south to Waterman Street. Even in summer, when relatively few students are on campus, Thayer Street remains lively, cerebral, and youthful—there are coffeehouses, sandwiches shops, ethnic restaurants, bookstores, a few school buildings, and a decidedly countercultural buzz that befits the entertainment district nearest Brown; plenty of students from nearby RISD also hang out in these parts. When school's in session, expect to fight many Maynard Keynes–debating trust-funders for the alfresco tables.

FOX POINT AND INDIA POINT PARK

You'll find another corridor of artsy, student-frequented shops, eateries, and fair-trade cafés along the slightly less trafficked **Wickenden Street,** which runs east-west across Fox Point, at the southern end of College Hill fronting Providence Harbor. India Point, at the southeastern tip of this neighborhood, has for many years been the center of the city's Portuguese community, and because of its fine restaurants and shops it draws folks from all over. The crowd along Wickenden Street is less exclusively identified with Brown University—you'll find just as many RISD students as well as other teens and young adults from around the city.

Eighteen-acre India Point Park, accessible either from Exit 3 off I-195 or by heading south on Gano Street or South Main Street from Wickenden Street, provides the city's only frontage on Narragansett Bay, right at the bay's head where it meets the Seekonk and Providence Rivers. The northern terminus of the East Bay Bike Path, the park has a small network of paved trails suitable for biking or strolling, plus meadows ideal for tossing a ball or Frisbee.

At the west end of the neighborhood, South Water Street runs south along the east bank of the Providence River. There's a small park at the end and parking along the street, and from here you look down the river and see the hulking gates of the city's Hurricane Barrier, built in 1961–1966. Beyond it is the soaring arched truss of the bridge that carries the new "Iway"—the recently relocated I-195—over the bay. On the opposite side of the Providence River, via Globe Street, which is off Allens Avenue, you can get a closer look at the Hurricane Barrier, a roughly 700-foot-long structure whose massive doors are kept open except when the city is threatened by major storms; to date this has been only a handful of occasions.

NORTH AND EAST OF COLLEGE HILL

The lower slopes of College Hill to the north and east cover a substantial area, and while safe and pleasant, it is more difficult to cover on foot than College Hill, Wickenden Street, and downtown. You might consider driving or taking a bus to Blackstone Boulevard or Blackstone Park and then walking, or consider riding a bike through this area—it's one of the few neighborhoods within Providence city limits that's highly conducive to cycling.

North of the intersection with Wickenden Street, Hope Street has several cool shops and eateries, plus some fine old homes. A few blocks north of Wickenden Street is the **Rhode Island Historical Society Library** (121 Hope St., 401/273-8107, www.rihs.org, 10 A.M.–5 P.M. Wed.–Fri., free), worth a stop if you have even a casual interest in genealogy or early state history. Documents pertaining to Rhode Island, including all manner of birth, death, and marriage records, date as far back as the days of Roger Williams. There are also prints, paintings, photos, and other historical items. The society sponsors 90-minute city walking tours July–mid-October with a focus on history, the waterfront, architecture, art, and similar topics.

A few more blocks up Hope Street, note the decadent **Governor Henry Lippitt House Museum** (199 Hope St., 401/453-0688, www.preserveri.org, tours 11 A.M.–2 P.M. Fri. or by appointment, $10). A sterling example of a high-style Italianate Victorian mansion from the 1860s, the building reveals the fine craftsmanship of the day with ornately carved Renaissance revival woodwork, meticulous stencil work, and myriad faux finishes. Even if you have little interest in interior design and restoration, the Lippitt Museum is a must-see. Many of the furnishings in the house belonged to Lippitt family members, and the museum periodically throws events, teas, and dinners that offer an intimate glimpse into life in this house during the Victorian era.

Another block north, at Lloyd Avenue, you'll pass by the prestigious **Moses Brown School** (250 Lloyd Ave., 401/831-7350, www.moses-brown.org), a Quaker prep school notable for its tree-shaded lawns and fine old buildings that has been here since 1784. You can visit the **Krause Gallery** (Jenks Center, Friends Hall, www.mosesbrown.org/krausegallery, 8 A.M.–4 P.M. Mon.–Fri., free), which shows the works of noted local and national sculptors, painters, and photographers.

Farther down Angell Street, past the enormous Brown University Athletic Complex, is a short strip of shops and a handful of cheap eateries, including the engaging **Books on the Square** (471 Angell St., 401/331-9097, www.booksq.com) which has a lively café and is a great place for a break or book shopping. This tiny commercial district, **Wayland Square**, serves the many residential blocks nearby, home to young professionals, students, and faculty of Brown, RISD, and the city's other universities.

Blackstone Boulevard

Farther east down Angell Street past Butler Avenue is the hilly 40-acre **Blackstone Park,** a grassy, tree-shaded park ideal for a stroll. It has a couple of ponds and several walking paths, plus some nice spots for a picnic. The mostly upper-middle-class residential neighborhood surrounding the park contains many fine stucco, wood-frame, and redbrick homes from the early part of the 20th century, all with neat gardens and perfectly manicured lawns.

From the northern end of Blackstone Park, west down Irving Avenue is the southern end of Blackstone Boulevard, a broad tree-lined avenue with a wide grassy median that's usually abuzz with joggers, walkers, inline skaters, and cyclists. A little more than a mile north on Blackstone Boulevard, on the right, is the entrance to the gracious 210-acre **Swan Point Cemetery** (585 Blackstone Blvd., 401/272-1314, http://swanpointcemetery.com), laid out in 1875. This is one of the country's foremost garden cemeteries, and visitors are encouraged to bicycle (slowly), walk, or drive the grounds, which are laced with beautiful gardens. Among the famous Rhode Islanders buried here are horror writer H. P. Lovecraft and Civil War general Ambrose Burnside.

A short distance north along Blackstone Boulevard is **Lippitt Memorial Park,** a pretty little slice of greenery with a grand old central fountain and ample seating. The jogging path up the median of Blackstone Boulevard terminates where Hope Street becomes East Avenue, almost suspiciously across the street from **Maximillian's Ice Cream Cafe** (1074 Hope St., 401/273-7230). At this point you're a short walk from Providence's northeastern border with Pawtucket—this is a part of Providence many visitors never see, and yet it's extremely charming and diverse. Yuppies, families, gays and lesbians, and students and academics have settled here, taking advantage of the low-key and quiet pace still close to bustling downtown.

CRANSTON STREET ARMORY

Much of the rest of Providence—the neighborhoods south, west, and northwest of downtown—is dominated by lower-income residential neighborhoods and industry. One particularly fascinating site just southwest of downtown is the Cranston Street Armory (125 Dexter St.), a massive 1907 yellow-brick and granite building that housed the Rhode Island

National Guard for many years but is now threatened with demolition. This centerpiece of the gradually gentrifying West Broadway neighborhood is on the National Trust for Historic Preservation's list of most endangered structures. Much talk has centered on turning the building into a state-of-the-art performing arts center; so far, however, it has been rehabilitated piecemeal as state funds allow, including transforming some of the towers into office space for government agencies. This neighborhood has enormous potential, with many striking, but often dilapidated, Victorian homes, including many examples of Second Empire and Greek Revival styles.

ROGER WILLIAMS PARK

You'll want to drive or take the bus the roughly four miles south of downtown to reach the city's largest and most treasured urban oasis, 430-acre Roger Williams Park (Elmwood Ave., 401/785-3510, grounds 9 A.M.–9 P.M. daily), the home of Roger Williams Park Zoo. Visitors can bike, skate, or walk nearly 10 miles of paved roads (open to auto traffic, but only at low speeds, and there's usually ample room for all people and vehicles to maneuver). Unpaved trails also meander into the verdant greenery around the 10 lakes (many where you can rent small boats). The great-great-granddaughter of Roger Williams, Betsey Williams, donated the land for this park in the 1870s, and it retains its splendid Victorian layout, created by designer Horace W. S. Cleveland in 1878. The look and ambience borrows heavily from the most famous of 19th-century park designers, Frederick Law Olmsted.

One of the most architecturally significant structures in the park, the imposing redbrick colonial revival **casino** dates to 1896. It has impressive views from its veranda over the restored music bandstand and Roosevelt Lake. With a ballroom crowned by 20-foot ceilings and ornate plaster friezes and trim, it is a fine example of the park's success in restoration and a favorite place for weddings and parties. Surrounding the casino and extending throughout several parts of the park are lovely rose and flower gardens as well as a Japanese garden. The **Charles H. Smith Greenhouses** (11 A.M.–5 P.M. daily), which date to 1937, house cactus, rain forest, and herb gardens.

You can catch live music events at the **Benedict Temple to Music,** an amphitheater. Kids enjoy the reproduction vintage carousel at **Carousel Village** (11 A.M.–5 P.M. daily), which also has a miniature golf course, bumper boats, and other rides and amusements. You can also visit the **Betsey Williams Cottage** (1–4 P.M. Sun. mid-Apr.–mid-June and mid-Sept.–Oct.), a small history museum that preserves the legacy of the city's founding family.

Museum of Natural History

Roger Williams Park is home to the Museum of Natural History (401/785-9457, www.providenceri.com/museum, 10 A.M.–5 P.M. daily, museum $2, museum and planetarium $3), which contains a planetarium and more than 250,000 objects and artifacts collected during the past two centuries—at any given time, just 2 percent of the museum's holdings are on display. These include preserved mollusk shells, birds, mammals, rocks, minerals, and—a particular strength—fossils from the region's coal age. The museum displays cultural artifacts, mostly from North America, including baskets, textiles, tools, and carvings—but with significant representation from Africa, Oceana, and other parts of the world. Rotating exhibits are held every few months; a recent example is *Life of Stars: From Nebula to Supernova.* This grandiose but intriguing château-esque building dates to 1895 and was built by the firm Martin and Hall. The state's only museum of natural history, the museum has an impressive collection, but the overall feel and appearance of the place seems to be from another era—it's not a dynamic museum. Considerably more stimulating is the attached **Cormack Planetarium,** where a dazzling computerized star projector offers a memorable lesson in astronomy. The 35-minute shows are presented at 2 P.M. Saturday–Sunday November–June and at 2 P.M. daily July–October.

PROVIDENCE

[Roger Williams Park Zoo

The Roger Williams Park Zoo (1000 Elmwood Ave., 401/785-3510, www.rogerwilliamsparkzoo.org, 9 A.M.–4 P.M. daily year-round, $12 adults, $6 children) has more than 1,000 animals of more than 165 species. It's the third-oldest zoo in the nation, and, believe it or not, has been ranked among the nation's 10 best. It's currently in the midst of an ambitious restoration plan called "New Zoo" to make it even better. The Fabric of Africa habitat, which has elephants, Masai giraffes, zebras, and cheetahs, was expanded and renovated in 2008 to include new interpretive signage, more space for the animals, and a new viewing deck to get close to the animals. As of 2010, work was shifting to the North America habitat, where the polar bear exhibit is being expanded to eight times its previous size, along with new habitats for bald eagles and seals.

Other animals on display here include playful lemurs in the Madagascar habitat; moon bears and snow leopards along the Marco Polo Trail; and monkeys, sloths, and snakes inhabiting the Tropical America exhibit, a recreated rain forest accessed by a swaying rope bridge. Smaller but still very popular exhibits include the African Fishing Village, a farmyard petting zoo, the Natural Wetlands Trail, and the educational zoo laboratory.

Entertainment and Events

NIGHTLIFE

Students, students, students…need anybody say more? They're everywhere you look, and they've created a vibrant market for pulsing nightclubs, swanky lounges, and singles joints. Providence also has the usual dive bars, with regular joes quaffing Bud tall boys, smoking Marlboro Lights, shooting pool, sucking down buffalo wings, and watching *Monday Night Football*. But for a relatively small city, it also has a surprising number of high-profile, sophisticated, and in some cases snobby boîtes. Actual velvet ropes are the exception rather than the rule, but a number of bars in this town set up invisible velvet ropes—if you don't fit the look or the style, you may feel rather left out.

Downcity and in the adjoining Jewelry District are the greatest concentration of the city's nightspots, including big and brawny dance clubs that simmer with the libidos of drunken college kids and revelers from the suburbs along with cool live-music clubs drawing the latest and strangest alternative rock and jazz acts. Providence also has a thriving gay scene, with several extremely popular clubs that pull in patrons from all over southern New England along with the many lesbian and gay students in town.

Hangouts

For pre- or postdinner drinks with a special someone, consider the Westin Providence's plush **Fleming's Steakhouse and Wine Bar** (1 W. Exchange St., 401/598-8000). Even if you're not a fan of hotel bars, you might give this upscale, inviting bar a chance—it's close to everything downtown, and the menu of fine wines and drinks is impressive. Keep in mind that it's also a favorite of cigar smokers.

Monet Dance Lounge (115 Harris Ave., 401/351-4848) is a classy alternative to the bump and grind of club life. Both indoor and outdoor space allows plenty of room to dance, and VIP sections give you star-worthy treatment.

Blake's Tavern (122 Washington St., 401/274-1230, www.blakestavern.com, 11 A.M.–1 A.M. daily) draws the after-work set for cocktails and tasty bar fare—wings, nachos, and the like. **AS220** (115 Empire St., 401/861-9190) features an eclectic mix of entertainment, from poetry slams to comedy shows, with a crowd that's just as diverse. **Liquid Lounge** (165 Angell St., 401/454-3434, 11:30 A.M.–1 A.M. Sun.–Thurs., 11:30 A.M.–2 A.M. Fri.–Sat.) is a sexy pickup spot off Thayer Street with a mostly Brown University crowd of arty countercultural types. Working professionals head straight from work to the **Tunnel Bar** (1 Cookson Pl., 401/421-4646), with a modern, cosmopolitan attitude that gets younger through the night. Among the several Irish pubs in the city, **Muldowney's** (103 Empire St., 401/831-6202, 10 A.M.–1 A.M. Mon.–Thurs., 10 A.M.–2 A.M. Fri.–Sat., noon–1 A.M. Sun.) scores significant crowds because of its proximity to AS220.

Suave and romantic **L'Elizabeth** (285 S. Main St., 401/861-1974, 11 A.M.–1 A.M. daily) is a sit-down bar pouring international coffees, single malts, cognacs, and similar after-dinner treats in a lavish drawing room of armchairs and sofas; soft jazz is piped in, and a handful of desserts are offered, including a delicious white-chocolate cheesecake. In the Jewelry District, young and old convene for jukebox tunes and Pabst Blue Ribbon at **Nick-a-Nee's** (75 South St., 401/861-7290, 3 P.M.–1 A.M. Sun.–Thurs., 3 P.M.–2 A.M. Fri.–Sat.), which hosts pool tournaments on Tuesday and Saturday nights.

At Providence Place Mall, you'll find a 40,000-square-foot branch of the national shrine to grown-ups who refuse to grow up: **Dave and Buster's** (401/270-4555, www.daveandbusters.com, 11:30 A.M.–midnight Sun.–Wed., 11:30 A.M.–1 A.M. Thurs.–Sat.) pulses with the sounds of high-tech video games and similar amusements; there's a huge bar, the crowd likes to party, and they party late. At **Snookers** (53 Ashburton St., 401/351-7665, www.snookersri.com, 11:30 A.M.–1 A.M. Sun.–Thurs., 11:30 A.M.–2 A.M. Fri.–Sat.), shoot pool to your heart's content—this sprawling place has many tables.

Live Music and Clubs

The city's main venue for major touring music acts is the **Dunkin' Donuts Center** (1 LaSalle Sq., at Broadway and Atwells Ave., 401/331-6700), in the western end of downtown. Down toward Fox Point, **Fish Co.** (515 S. Water St., 401/841-5510) pulls in a mix of local and nationally known alternative and rock music acts, playing mostly to a collegiate crowd. It's also a big draw for happy hour earlier in the evening.

At **Club Hell** (73 Richmond St., 401/351-1977), you'll find the city's Goth scene, where the pierced black-eyeliner set convenes to hang out. The sceney Federal Hill restaurant **Mediterreaneo** (134 Atwells Ave., 401/331-7760, www.mediterraneocaffe.com, 11:30 A.M.–9 P.M. daily) also has a dressy and rather exclusive nightclub where you'll hear mostly a Latin beat—that is, if you're able to get in; it's a very cliquey place. In the Jewelry District, the **Hi-Hat** (3 Davol Sq., 401/453-6500, www.thehihat.com, 4 P.M.–1 A.M. Tues.–Thurs., 4 P.M.–2 A.M. Fri., 5 P.M.–2 A.M. Sat.) offers live jazz, R&B, Latin, blues, and other cool beats in an attractive, urbane space.

Downtown, **Lupo's Heartbreak Hotel** (239 Westminster St., 401/331-LUPO—401/331-5876) is one of the top music venues in the city, booking rock, folk, country, and blues. **Ultra** (172 Pine St., 401/454-LIVE—401/454-5483) is one of the hottest spots in town for hip-hop beats, boasting the ultimate dance party complete with platforms and VIP tables. Look to **Safari Lounge** (103 Eddy St., no phone) for the latest underground, thrash, and punk acts.

Suburbanites and college students from schools throughout Rhode Island make the drive into the city to cut loose at **Jerky's** (71 Richmond St., 401/621-2244) for a night of cheap food, drinks, and pool. A bit of a dive bar, this is the place to go if you would rather wear jeans and flannel. If you're more the clubbing type, try **Art Bar** (171 Chestnut St., 401/272-0177, www.artbarprovidenceri.com/1.html), the original 25-and-over party spot for locals and vacationers alike. Music varies from past favorites to current hits, and Saturday all-request nights guarantee something for everyone.

Gay and Lesbian

Girlspot (150 Point St., 401/751-7166) is a terrific women's club that has a large dance floor, lots of nooks for sitting and talking, and friendly staff. A handsome bi-level space close to the bevy of straight and wild discos on Richmond Street, **Mirabar** (35 Richmond St.,

401/331-6761) is the definitive men's stand-and-model bar with a small dance floor and a cozier cocktail bar with a pool table upstairs. It tends to draw a fairly young and professional crowd.

Dark Lady (124 Snow St., 401/274-6620), on a desolate side street on the edge of downtown, is an appropriately shady location for a hard-core cruisy disco and hangout popular with leather men and other butch types.

THE ARTS

Providence enjoys a highly developed and richly endowed performing arts scene, with a slew of

GALLERY-HOPPING IN PROVIDENCE

Providence has an impressive fine arts scene, with galleries throughout downtown and College Hill. Among the better-known downtown venues is one at the historic Arcade: **Center-City Contemporary Arts** (65 Weybosset St., 401/521-2990), which focuses primarily on the works of Rhode Island artists. Also worth checking out is the **Stanley Weiss Collection** (292 Westminster St., 401/272-3200, www.stanleyweiss.com), known throughout the Northeast for its phenomenal selection of museum-quality antiques and silver jewelry and accessories. One of the most innovative and popular spaces in the city is **AS220** (115 Empire St., 401/831-9327), which is also a very nice restaurant and a place to listen to readings and live music. The **Rhode Island Foundation Gallery** (1 Union Station, off Exchange Terr., 401/274-4564, www.rifoundation.org), a former cafeteria in the old Union Station, shows rotating art exhibits. The Rhode Island Foundation is a center for philanthropy that acts as a liaison between donors and recipients in the public and private sectors in education, health care, and the arts. Works shown in the gallery focus heavily on local artists in all media.

On the East Side, a handful of galleries cluster around the Fox Point neighborhood, notably the **Peaceable Kingdom** (116 Ives St., 401/351-3472), where you'll find carved masks and figurines, lavish textiles, and paintings from around the world. Farther west on Wickenden Street you'll find **JRS Fine Art** (218 Wickenden St., 401/331-4380), which represents a number of reputable painters and potters, and **Picture This** (158 Wickenden St., 401/273-7263, www.picturethisgalleries.com), a respected frame and print shop. Down by India Point is **Bert Gallery** (540 S. Water St., 401/751-2628), whose paintings are mostly by notable 19th-early-20th-century Rhode Island artists (it's an excellent place to get a lesson in local art history). Finally, there are two spots near RISD and Brown: the **David Charles Gallery** (263 S. Main St., 401/421-6764), which has fine maritime art, beautiful framed photos of the Providence skyline, and numerous depictions of noted New England landmarks; and the historic **Providence Art Club** (11 Thomas St., 401/331-1114). This is the country's second-oldest art club — it occupies the 1790 Obadiah Brown House, where members still carry out the tradition of munching on jonnycakes in the vintage dining rooms.

The third Thursday of every month 5-9 P.M., the city sponsors a free **Gallery Night** (401/751-2628, www.gallerynight.info). you can ride one of three trolleys, which depart from Citizens Bank (1 Citizens Plaza), on a historic loop through downtown and the East Side, stopping at about 25 art galleries and museums. On hand to mingle with visitors at most of these events are local artists and gallery owners. Each of the three trolleys plies a different route — one through the East Side, one through the West Side, and one making the entire loop. On board, volunteer guides from the Providence Preservation Society offer commentary on the sights and neighborhoods along the way. Sakonnet Vineyards donates free wine (and other refreshments are also provided), and there's live music at some venues. Keep in mind that Rhode Island has lifted sales tax on all galleries within Providence's downtown arts district — which means you'll find some very good art buys in these parts.

theaters that range from big-time showcases of pre-Broadway shows and national touring acts to inexpensive avant-garde local workshops that will challenge your sensibilities. It's a good destination for people who like to take chances—there's no shortage of educated and progressive, even a bit jaded, audiences. Not an evening passes in Providence without the opportunity to watch some out-there abstract dance piece, catch an obscure foreign film at one of the art cinemas, or see a courageous new dramatic work by the next wunderkind in the city's theater scene.

You can look to the city's colleges for a wide range of dance, theater, music, and other arts performances, with **Rhode Island College** (600 Mt. Pleasant Ave., www.ric.edu/perf_arts) offering some of the best works. It's always worth checking its website to see what's playing and where; visit the school's Bannister Gallery for rotating art exhibits. On the city's West Side, this school doesn't always get the same attention as some of Providence's larger educational institutions, but its arts program is notable.

Also check to see what's happening at **Providence College** (401/865-2218, www.providence.edu), whose Blackfriars Theatre produces some first-rate plays. At **Brown University** (www.brown.edu), the acclaimed music department presents concerts in a wide range of disciplines, from chamber music to jazz. Plays and other performing arts are scheduled regularly at the school's **Dill Performing Arts Center** (77 Waterman St., 401/863-2838).

Theater

The **Providence Performing Arts Center** (220 Weybosset St., 401/421-2787, www.ppacri.org) ranks among New England's top venues for concerts, children's theater, and Broadway-style musical comedies—plus ballet, opera, and classical music. Throughout the year, top recording stars and a smattering of comedians such as Diana Krall, David Sedaris, and the swoon-inducing Jonas Brothers perform here. In recent years Broadway and national-touring musicals have included *The Scarlet Pimpernel, Godspell,* and *Annie,* while

© MICHAEL BLANDING

AS220 offers a peek into Providence's diverse arts scene.

Cinderella and *Sesame Street Live* have graced the children's stage.

One of the city's most innovative venues for all kinds of arts, **AS220** (115 Empire St., 401/831-9327, www.as220.org) has cultivated a following for undiscovered and experimental works. It occupies a large space with numerous artists-in-residence, and it's home of various local theater groups, including the edgy **Perishable Theatre** (95 Empire St., 401/331-2695, www.perishable.org), which produces cutting-edge plays.

Another major key to the gentrification of the once-seedy Westminster Street area, the **Providence Black Repertory Company** (276 Westminster St., 401/351-0353, www.blackrep.org) formed in 1996 to help promote and celebrate the theatrical contributions of black dramatists, actors, and other performers. In addition to staging plays, this acclaimed theater hosts open-mike nights, discussions, readings, and music.

The Tony Award–winning **Trinity Repertory Company** (201 Washington St., 401/351-4242, www.trinityrep.com) presents seven classic and contemporary plays annually with a season running September–June. They also put on an annual holiday production of *A Christmas Carol.*

Music and Dance

The **Rhode Island Philharmonic** (667 Waterman Ave., East Providence, 401/242-7070, www.ri-philharmonic.org) has been a cultural mainstay in Providence since 1945, pulling in notable guest conductors from time to time, plus artists such as Debbie Reynolds and Marvin Hamlisch. The Philharmonic presents a classical series, three fully staged operas, a pop series, and several family-oriented pieces. The Lincoln-based modern-dance rep company **Fusionworks** (401/946-0607, www.fusionworksdance.org) performs at venues throughout the state and elsewhere in the Northeast.

Film

Try to catch a movie at the **Avon Cinema** (260 Thayer St., 401/421-0020, www.avoncinema. com), which shows both popular and art movies (and serves Häagen-Dazs), with midnight screenings some nights. Another art house is the **Cable Car Cinema** (204 S. Main St., 401/272-3970, www.cablecarcinema.com). At Providence Place Mall you'll find the 16-screen **Providence Place Cinemas 16** (800/315-4000) and the **IMAX theater** (www.imax. com), which shows larger-than-life features on a six-story screen with a mind-blowing (perhaps ear-splitting) 12,000-watt surround-sound system.

FESTIVALS AND EVENTS
Summer

In mid-June, one of Providence's most vibrant ethnic communities throws an **Annual Cape Verdean Independence Day Celebration** (India Point Park, 401/222-4133), which gives attendees a chance to sample authentic Cape Verdean foods, observe arts and crafts exhibits, and listen to music and storytelling. Also in June, Providence's dynamic gay and lesbian community celebrates **RI Pride Fest** (401/467-2130, www.prideri.com) at

Station Park, just opposite Providence Place Mall. In early August, foodies descend on the **Best of Rhode Island Party** (Rhode Island Convention Center, 401/781-1611), during which more than 80 winners of *Rhode Island Monthly* magazine's "best of" food awards dole out portions of the grub that made them so popular. Begun in 1997, the **Rhode Island International Film Festival** (various locations in Providence and neighboring towns, 401/861-4445, www.rifilmfest.org) has grown into a highly prestigious event showing more than 265 films; it's held every August.

Fall

In the middle of September, about 30 of the city's ethnic communities gather for the **Annual Rhode Island Heritage Festival** (Roger Williams National Memorial, North Main St., 401/222-4133, www.preservation.ri.gov/heritage) to share traditional song and dance, arts and crafts demonstrations, and foods. In early November, bring out your inner decorator at the **Annual Fine Furnishings–Providence** (Rhode Island Convention Center, 401/816-0963, www.finefurnishingsshow.com), which focuses mostly on the handcrafted furnishings and decorative arts of New England artisans. You'll find a nice range of both traditional and contemporary wares in all price ranges.

Winter and Spring

Like many U.S. cities, Providence ushers in the new year with **Bright Night** (various sites downtown, 401/351-2596, www.brightnight. org), with family-oriented theater, music, art, and dance performances. Yachting and sailing enthusiasts gear up for the coming season in mid-January at the **Providence Boat Show** (Rhode Island Convention Center and Dunkin' Donuts Center, 401/846-1115, www. providenceboatshow.com), where dealers show off the latest sailboats, powerboats, and equipment. A week later at the same venue, you can hunt for cars at the **Northeast International Auto Show** (Rhode Island Convention Center, 717/671-4300, www.motortrendautoshows.com/providence). In mid-February, the convention center hosts the **Rhode Island Spring Flower and Garden Show** (401/272-0980, www.flowershow.com). Later in February the convention center is the site first of the **RV and Camping Show** (401/458-6000); a week later the **Southeastern New England Home Show** (401/438-7400, www.ribahomeshow.com); and in early February the **Rhode Island Pet Show and the International Cat Association (TICA) Cat Show** (800/955-7469, www.jenksproductions.com). One of the most popular events at the convention center is the **Business Expo** (401/521-5000), which comes in late April and hosts about 400 exhibitors and dozens of professional development workshops.

Shopping

For several reasons, Providence offers an uncharacteristically good selection of unusual shops along with the chains you'd find anywhere. First, a nice thing about the city's Gaps, Victoria's Secrets, and other chains: The vast majority are contained within one of the best-designed and best-situated urban shopping malls you'll ever find, Providence Place. This mammoth structure anchors downtown and overlooks the brilliantly landscaped riverfront, and it's close to several hotels and within walking distance of the universities. There are several good restaurants on the ground floor, plus a top-level food court that's better than most, as well as a movie theater and IMAX. If malls are often guilty of sucking the life out of cities and forcing people out to bland suburban retail compounds that could be anywhere, Providence Place at least draws people to the heart of downtown. That being said, independent-shop owners have had a tough go of it for the past few years, and many around the city have closed, especially on the East Side. There's some concern that the presence of Providence Place Mall and the emergence of so many chain businesses elsewhere have cost a number of indies too many customers for them to make a successful go of it.

Beyond the mall, Providence has a number of funky and hip design shops, galleries, art-supply stores, indie book and record shops, vintage clothiers, and home-furnishings and gift boutiques. These are geared as much toward visitors as they are to the city's artists, students, academics, and hipsters. Providence lures creative types, and these very people often end up opening offbeat and innovative businesses. And while this isn't necessarily an ideal city for bargain hunters, commercial rents are much, much lower than in Boston, New York City, Block Island, or Cape Cod. You'll often find decent deals on antiques and art, and at the student-oriented spots you'll have no trouble homing in on discount threads, used books and CDs, and low-priced bric-a-brac.

PROVIDENCE PLACE MALL

Opened in 1999, Providence Place Mall (1 Providence Pl., 401/270-1000, www.providenceplace.com, 10 A.M.–9 P.M. Mon.–Sat., noon–6 P.M. Sun.) is an immense four-story atrium mall with a 16-screen Showcase Cinema multiplex and an IMAX theater along with a fairly standard upscale mix of apparel, home-furnishing, and other chain shops. The top-floor 700-seat food court is unusually good, with Ben and Jerry's, Johnny Rockets, Subway, Japanese and sushi that's excellent by mall standards, Italian, and Chinese eateries. The ground level is lined with sit-down restaurants that are mostly upscale-looking if not genuinely expensive; most of them are jam-packed on weekend evenings. The mall has been successful in drawing visitors from the burbs, but some question how much it has drawn people into the city—you can exit I-95 directly into the mall parking garages, barely touching city surface streets. On the other hand, the mall is within walking distance of the riverfront, State House, convention center, and even College Hill—especially on warm days, plenty of shoppers wander out and explore the city. Major shops include Filene's, Lord and Taylor, and Nordstrom (which draws plenty of bargain-hunters from Massachusetts, which strangely enough lacks a Nordstrom). You'll also find chain shops such as Abercrombie and Fitch, Aveda, J. Jill, Restoration Hardware, Bed Bath & Beyond, Brooks Brothers, J. Crew, Lindt, Yankee Candle, Borders, Ann Taylor Loft, and all the myriad siblings in the ubiquitous Gap family—about 150 stores total.

DOWNTOWN

Apart from Providence Place Mall, downtown's most engaging retail spots are scattered about, in many cases down quiet little streets where you might not expect to find anything. If shopping is a sport to you, it's worth covering downtown block by block to discover its gems.

For unique scores, be sure to check out **Copacetic** (17 Peck St., 401/273-0470, www.copaceticjewelry.com, 10 A.M.–6 P.M. Mon.–Fri., 10 A.M.–4 P.M. Sat.), where you'll find a colorful array of clever, if at times surreal, jewelry, clocks, candlesticks, and other cool handcrafted accoutrements. RISD students and other arts-and-crafts aficionados frequent the **Jerry's Artarama** (14 Imperial Pl., 401/331-4530, 10 A.M.–6 P.M. Mon.–Sat., noon–4 P.M. Sun.), set in an imposing old knife factory that is also the site of CAV restaurant on a quiet side street in the Jewelry District.

Cellar Stories Bookstore (111 Mathewson St., 401/521-2665, www.cellarstories.com, 10 A.M.–6 P.M. Mon.–Sat.) is the largest used and antiquarian bookstore in the state, specializing not only in hard-to-find and out-of-print books but also magazines and periodicals.

Westminster Street is becoming a hotbed of design shops, among them **Homestyle Abode** (229 Westminster St., 401/277-1159), which carries cool housewares, gifts, home accessories, and furnishings; and **Design Within Reach** (210 Westminster St., 401/831-1452, www.dwr.com, 10 A.M.–6 P.M. Mon.–Sat., noon–5 P.M. Sun.), an interior design studio that carries wonderful furniture.

THE EAST SIDE

Several commercial strips are on the East Side, beginning at the base of College Hill along North and South Main Streets, and also in the Brown University retail corridor along Thayer Street. Wickenden Street, at the southern tip of the East Side, also makes for great window-shopping, and you'll find a small but lively district around Wayland Square, just east of Brown University and Hope Street.

Don't be alarmed by the unusually friendly staff of the fine men's clothier **Marc Allen** (200 S. Main St., 401/453-0025). This upscale shop has been a favorite for business and sports suits since the 1940s and still makes personalized service and superlative-quality clothing a priority.

With art students strolling around every corner, it's no surprise that Providence has some excellent sources for supplies, including most prominently the **RISD Store** (30 N. Main St., 401/454-6464, www.risdstore.com, 8:30 A.M.–7 P.M. Mon.–Fri., 10 A.M.–5 P.M. Sat.–Sun.), which also has one of the best selections of art books and periodicals in the city. It's fitting that Providence would have several exceptional jewelry stores—among the best known is **Martina and Company** (120 N. Main St., 401/351-0968, www.martina-company.com, 11 A.M.–6 P.M. Tues.–Wed. and Fri., 11 A.M.–7 P.M. Thurs., 10 A.M.–5 P.M. Sat.), a contemporary gallery that occupies a dramatic space. Meanwhile, edgy and cool but very wearable women's clothing are the draw at **Capucine** (359 S. Main St., 401/273-6622, noon–4 P.M. Mon., 11 A.M.–6 P.M. Tues.–Fri., 11 A.M.–5 P.M. Sat.), a magnet for style-conscious hipsters.

Wickenden Street has a few good antiques stores, including the whimsically named **This and That Shoppe** (236 Wickenden St., 401/861-1394), a multiple-dealer establishment with about 50 sellers. Most of the businesses along this funky stretch, including the scads of eateries, are set in wood-frame and brick Victorians and a few colonials. Just off Wickenden Street, **Rustigian Rugs** (1 Governor St., 401/751-5100, www.rustigianrugs.com, 10 A.M.–5:30 P.M. Mon.–Fri., 10 A.M.–5 P.M. Sat.) has an astounding selection of fine rugs, mostly from Far Eastern and Middle Eastern locales. Where there are college students, you can always find used CDs—among several shops in town, **Round Again Records** (278 Wickenden St., 401/351-6292, www.roundagainrecordsri. com, 11 A.M.–6 P.M. Mon.–Fri., 11 A.M.–5 P.M. Sat.) ranks among the best.

In trendy Wayland Square, check out **Books on the Square** (471 Angell St., 401/331-9097, www.booksq.com, 9 A.M.–9 P.M. Mon.–Sat., 10 A.M.–6 P.M. Sun.), which has a broad selection of fiction and nonfiction and is particularly strong on feminist, gay and lesbian, political, and children's books. You can sit in a comfy armchair and flip through books before buying them. **Comina** (201 Wayland Ave., 401/273-4522, www.comina.com, 10 A.M.–5:30 P.M. Mon.–Sat., noon–4 P.M. Sun.) is a delightful home-furnishings shop with emphasis on country British and French furnishings.

The comprehensive **Brown University Bookstore** (244 Thayer St., 401/863-3168, http://bookstore.brown.edu, 7:30 A.M.–8 P.M. Mon.–Fri., 10 A.M.–8 P.M. Sat., 10 A.M.–6 P.M. Sun.) also sells college sweatshirts and other logo items. Since you're in the jewelry capital of the nation, you might want to poke your head inside **Details** (277 Thayer St., 401/751-1870, 10:30 A.M.–7 P.M. daily), a top purveyor of both high-end and less pricey costume pieces of all kinds and styles. You'll find everything from handmade semiprecious beaded necklaces to crystal chandelier earrings. A funky local favorite, **Oop!** (220 Westminster St., 401/270-4366, www.oopstuff.com, 10 A.M.–7 P.M. Mon.–Sat., noon–5 P.M. Sun.) offers a cool range of home furnishings that includes a distinctive line of rustic furniture fashioned out of sticks along with gifts, objets d'art, toys, crafts, and jewelry, much of it made locally. The reputation is for fun, fairly inexpensive items, but Oop! sells some pricier antiques. The management has keen marketing sense, presenting all kinds of themed events, from free face-painting days to birthday parties celebrating stars such as Judy Garland and Mick Jagger. Despite the chain stores overtaking the neighborhood, there are still several excellent indie-owned eateries, boutiques, and shops, plus a great movie theater.

Up Hope Street, check out **Green River Silver Co.** (735 Hope St., 401/621-9092, www. greenriversilver.com, 10 A.M.–6 P.M. Mon.–Sat., 11 A.M.–4 P.M. Sun.), which custom-makes fine sterling-silver jewelry. **Studio Hop** (810 Hope St., 401/621-2262, 10 A.M.–6 P.M. Mon.–Sat., noon–5 P.M. Sun.) carries a wide and unusual range of gifts from all over the world, including Asian and Mediterranean skin care and beauty products, candles, framed photos and artwork, carved wooden bowls and utensils, and other hand-crafted items. The whimsical **Frog and Toad** (795 Hope St., 401/831-3434, 10 A.M.–6 P.M. Mon.–Sat., 11 A.M.–4 P.M. Sun.) stocks beaded jewelry, specialty soaps, funky imported furniture and crafts, and lush plants and topiaries.

Sports and Recreation

By virtue of being such a hilly city, merely maneuvering around Providence on foot qualifies as a recreational pursuit. Beyond that, within the city limits you'll find a smattering of venues for sports and enjoying the outdoors, but with so many large parks and recreation areas within a 15-mile radius, many residents get their exercise elsewhere. In addition to the activities described below, keep in mind the city's many exceptional parks, including Roger Williams Park, India Point Park, and Blackstone Park.

BICYCLING, JOGGING, AND INLINE SKATING

There aren't any great spots for mountain biking within Providence city limits (although you'll find several good spots nearby), but the city does have some neat routes for conventional biking. Keep in mind that this is a busy city with narrow streets and a high volume of auto traffic, particularly on the East Side, and you'll have some very steep hills to contend with.

Joggers and inline skaters face some of the same issues but can enjoy one span that bikers will find less useful. Beginning either by the Capitol grounds or at nearby Providence Place Mall, you can enjoy a marvelous stroll along the restored riverfront, a two-mile loop if you take it all the way down to Bridge Street.

Within Providence, few roads seem better suited to cyclists, joggers, and inline skaters than wide, tree-lined Blackstone Boulevard, which runs about 1.5 miles from Hope Street south to Blackstone Park, past handsome old homes and the entrance to Swan Point Cemetery. You can make a nice triangular loop out of this area, using Blackstone Boulevard as one leg, Hope Street as the longer leg (it meets with Blackstone near the Pawtucket border), and any of the many cross streets closer to Brown University as the shorter leg.

From Providence you have access to the 14.5-mile **East Bay Bike Path** (www.eastbaybikepath.com), which begins at India Point Park. You can rent bikes at **Providence Bicycle** (725 Branch Ave., 401/331-6610, www.providencebicycle.com, 9:30 A.M.–8 P.M. Mon.–Thurs., 9:30 A.M.–6 P.M. Fri. and Sun., closed Sat.), which is in northern Providence but worth the trip if you're a devotee of cycling.

BOATING, CANOEING, AND KAYAKING

Although not the boating hub that Newport, the East Bay, or South County are, Providence does have some access points that lead directly into Narragansett Bay, including some excellent areas for kayaking. Unfortunately, there are no kayak or canoe rentals in town; you'll have to venture down to South County or East Bay for those. You can take sailing classes geared to all levels of ability and experience at the **Community Boating Center** (109 India St., India Point Park, 401/454-7245, www.communityboating.com, 9 A.M.–5 P.M. Mon.–Fri.), which

has a new boathouse and a fleet of about 50 boats.

GOLF

Donald Ross, known for designing municipal courses in cities throughout New England, laid out **Triggs Golf Course** (1533 Chalkstone Ave., 401/521-8460, http://triggs.us, 6:30 A.M.–dusk daily, $23 for 9 holes, $40 for 18 holes) in the 1930s. It's a relatively affordable, reasonably well-maintained course with cart and club rentals.

Goddard Park Beach Golf Course (at Goddard State Park, Ives Rd., 401/884-9834, 7:30 A.M.–7 P.M. daily, $12–14) is a nine-hole public course that's open mid-April–late November.

ICE-SKATING

A favorite spot in the winter (November–March) is the **Bank of America Skating Center** (Kennedy Plaza, Dorrance St. and Washington St., 401/331-5544, www.providenceskating.com), which has public skating several times daily. This outdoor rink, twice the size of the famous one in Rockefeller Center, anchors downtown Providence, right by the bus station and close to the Riverwalk—it's good fun as much for taking to the ice as it is for watching skaters on a brisk day. Late spring–early fall, the focus shifts to roller-skating. Year-round, lessons in both of these balancing arts are given; you can also rent equipment at the large pavilion and admission booth at the end of the rink, which has lockers, a pro shop, a snack bar, and some private party rooms that revelers sometimes rent for birthdays and special events.

SPECTATOR SPORTS

Providence itself has but one pro sports team, the **Providence Bruins** (401/273-5000, www.providencebruins.com), an American Hockey League farm club that's a feeder for the NHL's Boston Bruins. The season runs October–early April, and tickets cost $20–30. Games are held at the **Dunkin' Donuts Center** (1 LaSalle Sq., box office 401/331-6700).

With all the schools in Providence, you'd

think there would be more opportunities to catch live college sporting events, but few of these institutions have notable athletic programs. A major exception is **Providence College** (401/331-0700, http://friars.collegesports.com), whose Friars basketball team frequently ranks near the top of the Big East Basketball Conference. Games are held at the Dunkin' Donuts Center. The college's hockey team (401/865-2168) is also quite accomplished and plays at Schneider Arena (Admiral St. and Huxley St.).

Accommodations

When it comes to hotels, Providence is a seller's market. There simply aren't many properties given the city's size and rapidly growing popularity—the city has among the highest occupancy rates in the nation. Things are improving, however, as the Westin Providence recently expanded, and the upscale Marriott Renaissance chain recently renovated the elegant Masonic Temple, near Providence Place Mall and the Rhode Island State House, into a fine hotel. The city's hotels are uniformly excellent, most within walking distance of great shopping, dining, and culture. You'll also find several historic inns, from high-end luxury spots to a few that serve travelers on a somewhat limited budget. For truly affordable accommodations, however, you'll have to venture outside town to nearby Warwick or Pawtucket, or even as far as Woonsocket, Bristol, or across the border to Seekonk or Fall River, Massachusetts.

It's fairly easy to get in and out of Providence, so consider choosing a hotel in the outlying regions—after all, Rhode Island is a tiny state, so even communities in the Blackstone River Valley or the East Bay are relatively convenient for exploring the capital. Staying in one of these nearby areas might save you $50–100 per night for a room that's comparable to what you'll find in the city, depending on the time of year. Providence is a commercial, educational, and political hub—it hosts a fair number of conventions and can be especially busy on weekends during the school year and weekdays any time. Generally, the farther ahead you book a room, the better you'll do on the rate.

DOWNTOWN PROVIDENCE $100-150

The **Courtyard by Marriott Providence Downtown** (32 Exchange Terr., 401/272-1191 or 888/887-7955, www.courtyard.com, $139–199) closely resembles the historic tanbrick structures on Exchange Street beside it—aesthetically it's a marvelous property, and it couldn't be more conveniently situated. Predictably, the hotel has been phenomenally popular since it opened, with relatively reasonable rates for downtown but high for the Courtyard brand. The 216 guest rooms are large and airy, and many have unobstructed views of the State House, Providence Place Mall, and WaterPlace Park. All have free high-speed Internet access, two-line phones, and large work desks. Common amenities include a business center and library, an indoor pool with a hot tub, a fitness center, and a small café. It can get a little harried in the small lobby, but that's a minor quibble; it's an all-around excellent property.

The **C Providence Biltmore** (11 Dorrance St., 401/421-0700 or 800/294-7709, www.providencebiltmore.com, $149–189) dates to 1922 and is unquestionably the city's grande dame. Each of the 291 guest rooms is quite cushy, and 181 of them are suites with sitting areas. It has a full health club, a car-rental agency next door, and a very good restaurant (a branch of the acclaimed seafood chain McCormick and Schmick's), but it's the sense of history and the perfect location that draw most guests back again. The hotel is worth visiting just to admire the elaborate lobby with its soaring three-tiered atrium, vaulted

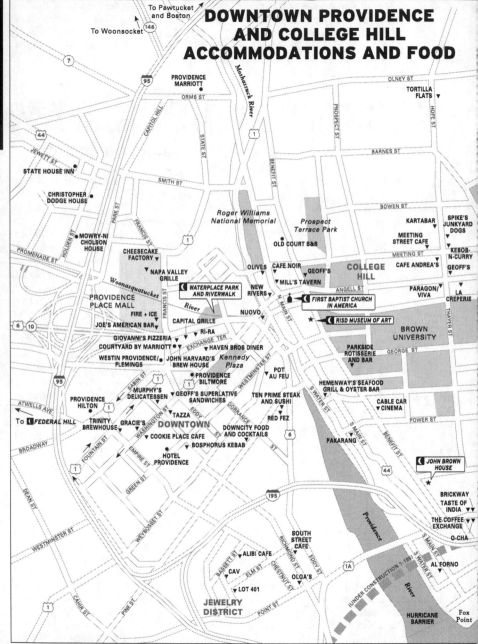

DOWNTOWN PROVIDENCE AND COLLEGE HILL ACCOMMODATIONS AND FOOD

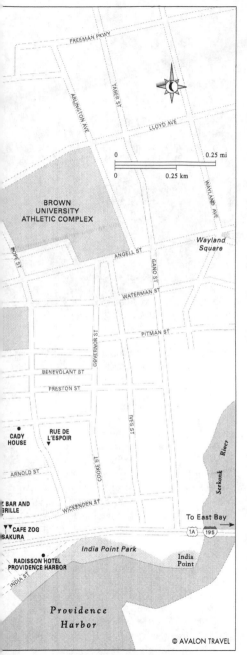

BROWN UNIVERSITY ATHLETIC COMPLEX

Wayland Square

FREEMAN PKWY

TABER ST

ARLINGTON AVE

LLOYD AVE

WAYLAND AVE

0   0.25 mi
0   0.25 km

HOPE ST

ANGELL ST

GANO ST

WATERMAN ST

GOVERNOR ST

PITMAN ST

BENEVOLANT ST

PRESTON ST

IVES ST

CADY HOUSE

RUE DE L'ESPOIR

COOKE ST

ARNOLD ST

BAR AND GRILLE

WICKENDEN ST

CAFE ZOG

SAKURA

Seekonk River

To East Bay

1A   195

India Point Park

India Point

RADISSON HOTEL PROVIDENCE HARBOR

INDIA ST

Providence Harbor

© AVALON TRAVEL

gilt ceiling, and gurgling fountains. At one time, the guest rooms had become somewhat less fabulous than the public areas, but an impressive and expensive $10 million rejuvenation in the early 2000s changed all that—accommodations are warm and atmospheric, with elegant bathroom fixtures, fine linens, and other cushy amenities. Fans of massage and facials should keep in mind that the Biltmore has a branch of the Red Door Spa.

Historic **Christopher Dodge House B&B** (11 W. Park St., 401/351-6111, www.providence-hotel.com, $130–180) occupies a gorgeously restored 1850s Italianate Victorian with a dignified redbrick facade, soaring pressed-tin ceilings, and beautifully crafted (and restored) original woodwork and plaster molding, tall windows, and polished wideplank floors. The eight-room property offers a nice range of rooms, the higher-end units with kitchenettes and some with gas fireplaces; all have a mix of inviting reproduction American antiques and contemporary conveniences, such as reading chairs and desks. Full breakfast and off-street parking are included, guests can use the close-by Foundry Sports Medicine and Fitness Center, and all rooms have cable TV and in-room phones. This is an upscale but relaxed property where you'll receive personal but unobtrusive service.

The 274-room **Providence Hilton** (21 Atwells Ave., at Broadway, 401/831-3900, $139–179), formerly a Holiday Inn, has been completely updated and upgraded with new textiles in all the rooms along with a full fitness center, an indoor pool, and a whirlpool tub. Despite the upgrade, this property is in a loud and rather unattractive location at a busy intersection west of the convention center, just off I-95. You can walk to downtown attractions and Johnson and Wales, and Federal Hill is just a short walk in the other direction. Rates are lowest on weekends, and at busy times they go up significantly.

$150-250

One of the trendiest spots on the city's lodging

scene, the boutiquey **⟪ Hotel Providence** (311 Westminster St., 401/861-8000 or 877/776-8430, www.thehotelprovidence.com $159–209) occupies a stunning late-19th-century building on formerly forlorn Westminster Street, now at the center of this downtown neighborhood's comeback. The 64 rooms and 16 suites are outfitted with tiger-maple furnishings, plush upholstered chairs and beddings (pillow-top beds, duvets and sheets with high thread counts), and original art by RISD Graduate School chair and acclaimed artist Nancy Friese. Each unit has a large work desk, a coffeemaker, a hair dryer, a shower with a rain showerhead, high-speed wireless Internet, dual phone lines with voicemail, a large TV, a CD player–clock radio, and top-quality bath amenities. This is a hip, design-themed hotel that has become a fashionable fixture of downtown Providence. It's very close to the Johnson and Wales downtown campus and all the bars and dining of the Jewelry District. The ground floor hosts one of the city's top restaurants, Aspire (formerly L'Epicureo).

Offering the only accommodations in the city's bustling Federal Hill neighborhood is the trendy **⟪ Hotel Dolce Villa** (63 De Pasquale Ave., 401/383-7031, www.dolcevillari.com, $169–309) on De Pasquale Square. Although this is a small operation with just 14 one- and two-bedroom suites, it's run like a full-service hotel, with a well-trained 24-hour staff and experienced management. A departure from the usual dark and heavy New England look, guest room decor feels distinctly contemporary, bright, and sleek, with stainless-steel appliances and white tile walls, white marble floors, linens, and modern furniture, including leather sofas; a few rooms have balconies overlooking the festive café culture in the square below. Every suite comes with a fully equipped kitchen, making this a true bargain—and a great nest to host dinner parties using ingredients from the fabulous food shops steps from the hotel. Other nice touches include DVD and CD players, flat-screen TVs, and, in the two-room suites, remote-control gas-burning fireplaces. Behind the main building, the hotel also rents out Villa Toscana, a spectacular VIP suite with two

The Hotel Providence is a highlight of Westminster Street.

bathrooms, a living room, an impressive commercial kitchen, and plenty of room to entertain (rates start at $499 per night for the villa). This superb little gem is operated by the restaurant group that owns the excellent Caffe Dolce Vita and Geppetto's Pizzeria next door and the nearby Mediterraneo Caffe.

The **Providence Marriott** (1 Orms St., 401/272-2400 or 886/807-2171, www.marriott.com, $169–209) has a superbly trained and extremely warm staff, plush rooms with desks and armchairs with ottomans, upscale bath amenities, a very nice health club and indoor-outdoor pool, and a good restaurant with a summer outdoor pool deck and grill, the Bluefin Grille (401/553-0424). Parking is also included. It's a terrific property in every regard but for the fact that it's slightly north of downtown's attractions and restaurants—a 10-minute walk, which is unpleasant only if it's cold or wet outside. This 351-room hotel is just a short walk north of the State House, however, and it's right off I-95.

Over $250

One of the most distinctive and admired contemporary hotels in downtown Providence is the 364-room **Westin Providence** (1 W. Exchange St., 401/598-8000 or 800/937-8461, www.westinprovidence.com, $270–300), a dramatic neoclassical skyscraper with peaked gables and a redbrick facade. Interior elements carry out the elegant theme, from the massive glass-dome rotunda to public areas of marble, polished dark woods, and recessed lighting. Guest rooms mix reproduction French and British antiques with rich fabrics and wallpapers, and the oversized bathrooms boast plush fixtures and fancy soaps and shampoos. Units in a level of rooms called Westin's Guest Office contain business-oriented perks such as ergonomically designed seating and desks, in-room fax machines, printers, and copiers, and two-line speakerphones. The rooftop health club, located on the sixth floor under a cavernous glass dome, ranks among the top health club facilities at any hotel in New England. It's available for $10 per day for nonguests, but has no fee for anyone staying at any Providence hotel. The hotel also has two restaurants, Flemings and Agora, and three lounges that have an extensive selection of cognacs, wines, and aperitifs. Another plus is the central location, with enclosed elevated walkways that connect the hotel both to the Providence Convention Center and Providence Place Mall. The Westin may lack the tradition of the nearby Biltmore, but in every other regard it's comparable or better.

COLLEGE HILL AND THE WATERFRONT
$100-150

Radisson Hotel Providence Harbor (220 India St., 401/272-5577 or 800/395-7046, www.radisson.com, $149–179), with 136 rooms and an enviable location overlooking Providence Harbor, is a very good mid-priced chain property that enjoys equal popularity among leisure and business travelers. Its location, wedged between I-195 and an exit ramp, may sound off-putting, but you can't beat the convenience to India Point Park, the hip restaurants on Wickenden Street and down by Fox Point, and the campuses of Brown and RISD. Rooms themselves are fairly traditional and cookie-cutter, but they are clean and bright, half have water views, and for an extra $10–20 you can get one with a whirlpool bath. It has an exercise room with whirlpool, an outdoor pool whose terrace has water views, and a functional restaurant.

The **C Old Court B&B** (144 Benefit St., 401/751-2002, www.oldcourt.com, $145–215) has just about the most wonderful setting in Providence, in the heart of the historic Benefit Street neighborhood. Built as a rectory in 1863, it's beside the old Rhode Island courthouse and nearly across from the original state house. Guest rooms have truly museum-quality antiques, collectibles, and chandeliers mostly from the Victorian era and early 20th century, and they are themed after specific styles or mood-setting furnishings: One room has Chippendale pieces, another Eastlake Victorian antiques. The Stove Room is anchored by an antique stove original to the rectory. The rooms are refreshingly free of clutter and cloying tchotchkes, allowing the inn to strike a pleasing balance between a traditional B&B and a small luxury hotel. This is one of the priciest B&Bs in inland Rhode Island, but considering the lavish furnishings, delightfully scenic and convenient location, and modern amenities (phones, TVs, and private baths in every room), the Old Court represents a very smart value.

Food

Providence had great restaurants well before Alice Waters and Wolfgang Puck began revolutionizing the way chefs approach cooking. The city has long been home to many ethnic groups with rich culinary traditions, including Italians, Portuguese, Latin Americans, and Asians. Providence's own Little Italy, on Federal Hill, ranks among the best in the world outside the big Italy. Indian and Thai restaurants flourished long before they became commonplace elsewhere, as did sushi. Seafood plays a vital role in local cuisine, and as an international port, Providence has always had access to exotic ingredients.

The city's arty element and throngs of students have created a desire, if not a need, for cheap and innovative foods—and don't forget, quite a few of those students and their professors are affiliated with the fabulous culinary arts program of Johnson and Wales University, home to the world's largest culinary archive.

As the trends of contemporary American cooking have evolved in recent years, from the garlic–mashed potato and sun-dried tomato phases of years gone by to today's obsession with kumquats, pomegranates, ostrich meat, and caramelized everything, Providence chefs have moved with the trends. The already exceptional seafood, Italian, Asian, and regional New England menus have been expanded and updated.

One of the more unusual ways to enjoy a bit of Rhode Island when you're miles away is to contact **Clambakes to Travel** (800/722-CLAM—800/722-2526, www.clambakeco.com), a Pawtucket-based company that will ship up to 16 authentic clambake meals anywhere in the continental United States. Each meal includes a 1.25-pound lobster, steamed clams, mussels, Portuguese *chouriço* sausage, corn on the cob, red bliss potatoes, and onions packed with rockweed inside a reusable pot. It's $123 for one meal but just $363 for six meals, which is a pretty reasonable price divvied up among a large group.

DOWNTOWN PROVIDENCE
Upscale

One of the most sought-after reservations for date-nighters, **New Rivers** (7 Steeple St., 401/751-0350, www.newriversrestaurant.com, 5–11 P.M. Mon.–Sat., $19–28) is an elegant, candlelit boîte housed in a 1793 warehouse originally built for iron merchants. The menu is as alluring as the atmosphere: The rabbit ravioli in sassafras *jus* with quail egg yolk and fava beans is a stunner, as is the grilled shoulder steak with peppercorn and coriander crust. Save room for the honey-drizzled Greek yogurt *panna cotta* in rhubarb consommé; you won't regret it.

A warm and romantic eatery in a quiet downtown alley, **Pot au Feu** (44 Custom House St., 401/273-8953, www.potaufeuri.com, 5–10:30 P.M. Sun.–Thurs., 5–11 P.M. Sat.–Sun., $16–23 in the bistro, $22–35 in the salon) is the city's seminal French restaurant. It opened in the early 1970s and has seemingly grown more popular each year. Depending on your mood or your budget, opt either for the classic bistro fare of the cozy basement space, where a classic bouillabaisse and a signature dessert of crème brûlée vie for your attention (dine here with a group of friends), or for the suave upstairs salon, which is good for celebrating a special occasion. Here try roast duckling, foie gras, and similarly rich French standbys.

The $25 prix fixe dinner menu is what pulls in value-loving gourmets to **Rue de L'Espoir** (99 Hope St., 401/751-8890, www.therue.com, 7:30 A.M.–10:30 P.M. Mon.–Fri and 8:30 A.M.–10:30 P.M. Sat.–Sun., $19–27). But it's the regular menu that they keep coming back for, with its specialties like delicate miso-glazed halibut and garlic-rubbed rib eyes.

Although it's a chain, the upscale **Capital Grille** (1 Union Station, 401/521-5600, 11:30 A.M.–11 P.M. daily, $25–45) feels distinctly local, a favorite haunt of politicos from the nearby State House and business execs from surrounding office buildings. The dry-aged porterhouse steaks are the main draw, plus broiled fresh lobster and obscenely large sides of baked potato, creamed spinach, and asparagus with hollandaise. The restaurant's interior has a dark, clubby feel, but that's part of the Capital Grille's gimmick. The entrance lies steps from Riverwalk and a very short distance from Providence Place Mall.

If you can pardon the mall location, the Providence branch of the upscale **Napa Valley Grille** (North Tower Entrance, Providence Place, 401/270-6272, 11:30 A.M.–9 P.M. daily, $17–33) works well as both an elegant setting for a special occasion and a spot for a tasty sampling of creative California-style cooking. Murals of the California wine country, wineglass chandeliers, and subdued amber lighting convey the theme, and the restaurant's wine list offers a nice balance of regional California wines. As for the menu, consider the crab-crusted Maine cod with zucchini noodles, Yukon gold potatoes, and orange-ginger sauce, or maple-walnut chicken breast with crème fraîche mashed potatoes, broccoli rabe, and a natural reduction.

Another of Providence's favorite power-lunch venues, **Nuovo** (1 Citizens Plaza, 401/421-2525, www.cafenuovo.com, 11 A.M.–10 P.M. Tues.–Sun., $24–40) presents an appropriately dazzling and extensive menu of rich and elaborate contemporary American dishes, including caramelized sea scallops, lamb-lobster ravioli, and a show-stopping Dover sole prepared at your table. The wine list reads like a who's who of top vintages. The restaurant occupies the ground floor of a fancy office tower at the confluence of the Moshassuck and Woonasquatucket Rivers—some seats are right on the river terrace.

Ten Prime Steak and Sushi (55 Pine St., 401/453-2333, www.tenprimesteakand-sushi.com, 5–10 P.M. Mon., 11:30 A.M.–10 P.M. Tues.–Thurs., 11:30 A.M.–11 P.M. Fri., 5–11 P.M. Sat.–Sun., $20–40) has been a white-hot culinary star for a decade, serving tasty portions of Asian-inspired steaks and seafood. The sushi is artful and delicious, but not every item has an Asian spin—a formidable

veal chop, for instance, is served with portobello mushrooms and shaved Parmesan. As interesting as the food is, Ten Prime has been most successful because of its lavish decor, huge fancy martinis, extensive sake list, and sexy attitude. Drawbacks are the occasionally haughty, or in some cases just flaky, service as well as certain dishes that sound interesting but are executed unevenly.

Creative but Casual

The fashionable Downcity option that caters to a see-and-be-seen crowd but is nevertheless totally unpretentious, **Gracie's** (194 Washington St., 401/272-7811, graciesprovidence.com, 5 P.M.–close Tues.–Sat., $11–40) is one of the city's favorite "special occasion" spots, known for its sterling service, inviting contemporary dining room, and exceptionally creative and well-crafted food that relies heavily on organic ingredients. You could kick things off with the unusual confit of frogs' legs, baby fennel, and roasted garlic before trying the entrée of roasted lamb loin with rhubarb, sweet potato puree, and *min jus*. There's always a superb tasting menu offered each day.

The quirky hangout **CAV** (14 Imperial Pl., 401/751-9164, www.cavrestaurant. com, 11:30 A.M.–10 P.M. Mon.–Thurs., 11:30 A.M.–1 A.M. Fri., 10 A.M.–10 P.M. Sat., 10:30 A.M.–10 P.M. Sun., $15–32) occupies an old knife factory in the Jewelry District and offers coffee, antiques, and victuals—the first letters of these three words spell the restaurant's name. So you can drop in to sip espresso and nosh on fresh baked goods or hunker down for a substantial meal, all the while checking out the considerable selection of vintage furnishings and goods. The menu tends toward fresh pastas, but a number of innovatively prepared fish and meat grills, salads, and desserts show up. CAV has folk and jazz music many weekend evenings. This is a popular spot—book ahead when possible.

You're likely to see culinary students from nearby Johnson and Wales congregating at the art deco **Downcity Food and Cocktails** (50 Weybosset St., 401/331-9217, www.

downcityfood.com, 11:30 A.M.–11 P.M. Mon.–Fri., 10 A.M.–11 P.M. Sat., 9 A.M.–11 P.M. Sun., $13–28), a stylish take on a traditional greasy spoon. The little cocktail bar has a following and is a favorite spot for an early drink; it's also a hot spot for brunch on Saturday and Sunday. Tasty dinner offerings include lobster-and-leek chowder with scallion-and-parsley crisps; roasted French rack of pork with apricot-guava glaze and mashed sweet and Idaho potatoes; and forest mushroom and port wine ravioletti with artichoke hearts, goat cheese, and arugula salad. There are great desserts too.

A quirky popular bistro serving mod-Californian cuisine, **Julian's** (318 Broadway, 401/861-1770, www.juliansprovidence.com, 9 A.M.–11 P.M. daily, $11–20) is a homey spot that offers uncomplicated, soul-warming fare that might include maple-walnut-pesto-crusted chicken breast with creamy potato salad and grilled pineapple, or ravioli with spinach, walnut, shallots, and goat cheese. The dining rooms are filled with unusual objets d'art and decorations. Breakfast is served all day—and the eggs Benedict Nova Scotia (with house-smoked salmon) is irresistible. At lunch, check out the long list of specialty sandwiches. BYOB.

The laid-back **Red Fez** (49 Peck St., 401/272-1212, lunch 11:30 A.M.–3:30 P.M. Tues.–Fri., dinner 5:30–10 P.M. Tues.–Thurs., 5:30–11 P.M. Fri.–Sat., $6–14) is a dark and intimate space that offers excellent light fare in the bar, including hefty and creative sandwiches, and more substantial dinners in a separate downstairs space, where you might sample orange-chipotle marinated pork tenderloin with seared kale and chipotle mashed sweet potatoes, or balsamic-glazed grilled salmon topped with tomato-caper relish served with grilled stuffed tomatoes and orzo-pesto salad.

Presenting healthful, creative, and truly eclectic cuisine that draws on Indian, Mediterranean, and East Asian ingredients and culinary traditions, **Lot 401** (44 Hospital St., 401/490-3980, from 5:30 P.M. Tues.–Sun., $18–28) definitely stretches when it comes to culinary innovation. Possibilities include Asian-braised pork bellies, or Atlantic cod with garlic, chives, flageolet beans, Chinese pork, and kale. This is a boisterous, see-and-be-seen place with a mod postindustrial aesthetic. It's in the Jewelry District and draws a young, fashionable crowd; the glitzy upstairs space becomes a swank night spot as the evening progresses.

Three Gringos CantinaMoJoe's (166 Broadway, 401/831-1183, 11 A.M.–9:30 P.M. daily, $8–18) is another of the cool Broadway spots. There's a great range of beers on tap and in bottles, and you can often catch cultural events here, including jewelry shows and art exhibits. It serves excellent grilled pizzas and other tasty comfort fare.

Pizza, Pasta, and Pub Grub

The loud, high-ceilinged **Cheesecake Factory** (94 Providence Pl., 401/270-4010, www.thecheesecakefactory.com, 11:30 A.M.–11 P.M. Mon.–Thurs., 11:30 A.M.–12:30 A.M. Fri.–Sat., 10 A.M.–11 P.M. Sun., $8–23) suffers a bit from crowds upon crowds (and that means obnoxiously long lines, especially on weekends), but the staff here takes it all in stride and remains consistently personable. If this seems like a lot of fuss for a national chain restaurant on the ground floor of a shopping mall, well, it is. Still, the many-paged menu suggests an amazing variety of foods, offering more appetizers than most restaurants have total items, plus pizzas, burgers, stir-fries, tacos, chicken and biscuits, pastas, seafood, steaks, and massive salads and sandwiches. Of course, plenty of people come simply for the cheesecake, which is available in about 35 varieties, from Dutch apple-caramel to lemon mousse.

Another of the popular chain eateries at Providence Place Mall, Boston-based **Joe's American Bar** (148 Providence Pl., 401/270-4737, www.joesamerican.com, 11 A.M.–11 P.M. Mon.–Thurs., 11 A.M.–midnight Fri.–Sat., 10 A.M.–10 P.M. Sun., $9–24) has a strong following for dependable—if rather predictable—comfort cooking favored by "regular joes" (and Janes): meat loaf flame-grilled with mashed potatoes and sautéed spinach, milk shakes, barbecued baby back ribs, and Cobb salads.

Vintage signs and memorabilia lend a festive air to **Ri-Ra** (50 Exchange Terr., 401/272-1953, www.rira.com, 11:30 A.M.–10 P.M. daily, $9–18), a dapper Irish eatery along Exchange Terrace. Try traditional standbys prepared with considerable flair, such as corned beef and cabbage, salmon boxty (charbroiled salmon with diced tomato, scallion, and cream cheese in a potato pancake with an Irish parsley sauce), and beef-and-Guinness stew—you'll find a smattering of vegetarian options as well. An oft-requested finale is Kelly's Cake, a dark-chocolate confection layered with Bailey's-chocolate mousse and coated with a milk-chocolate glaze. As you might guess, Ri-Ra is a hit with the after-work happy hour set.

Chicago-style pies are the specialty at the casual and kid-friendly **Giovanni's Pizzeria** (85 Richmond St., 401/621-8500, 11 A.M.–11 P.M. daily, $11–17). It's a favorite for the gooey, cheese-filled overstuffed calzones too.

An atmospheric subterranean haunt along Exchange Street, the **John Harvard's Brew House** (36 Exchange Terr., 401/274-BREW—401/274-2739, www.johnharvards.com, 11:30 A.M.–1 A.M. Sun.–Thurs., 11:30 A.M.–2 A.M. Fri.–Sat., $8–13) serves a fairly typical but reliable mix of pizzas, dinner salads, ale-battered fish-and-chips, hickory-smoked ribs, and more unusual foods such as baked crabmeat–stuffed cod over saffron rice with fresh corn, broccoli, and red pepper ragout.

Another favorite among fans of this genre, the **Trinity Brewhouse** (186 Fountain St., 401/453-BEER—401/453-2337, www.trinitybrewhouse.com, 11:30 A.M.–1 A.M. Mon.–Thurs., 11:30 A.M.–2 A.M. Fri., noon–2 A.M. Sat., noon–1 A.M. Sun., $8–22) brews several beers and serves an impressive range of snack foods and light entrées, including pulled-pork barbecue sandwiches and shepherd's pie. You'll find great burgers and also some veggie options such as falafel salad and margherita pizza.

Ethnic Fare

Look to **Bosphorus Kebab** (286 Westminster St., 401/454-3500, 11 A.M.–9 P.M. Fri.–Sat.,

11 A.M.–8 P.M. Sun., $3–7) for affordable and tasty Middle Eastern and Mediterranean victuals, including pizzas, salads, and freshly made soups.

Under the category of "eat-ertainment," **Fire and Ice** (48 Providence Pl., 401/270-4040, www.fire-ice.com, 11:30 A.M.–10 P.M. Mon.–Thurs., 11:30 A.M.–11 P.M. Fri.–Sat., 10 A.M.–10 P.M. Sun., dinner $17 all-you-can-eat, less for brunch and lunch) looks like a *Pee-wee's Playhouse* homage gone horribly awry, with dangling multicolored chandeliers and brilliantly hued furnishings of all shapes and sizes. Walk over to the various veggie, meat, and seafood stations, fill your bowl with whatever interests you (swordfish, pork, scallops, portobello mushrooms, leeks, or jalapeños), and then continue to a sauce station where again you get to pick (Jamaican jerk, rosemary, roasted corn and tomato, Thai basil cream, or a dozen others). Move on to a large grill, where you get to watch a chef cook your chosen ingredients. It's noisy and usually packed, but if the gimmick works for you, try it—there's no arguing that it's a great value for big eaters (return trips for extra helpings are included).

In the funky Broadway section, head to **Phoenix Dragon** (256 Broadway, 401/831-7555, www.phoenixdragonrestaurant.com, 11 A.M.–10 P.M. Mon.–Thurs., 11 A.M.–11 P.M. Fri.–Sat., 10:30 A.M.–9:30 P.M. Sun., $7–20) for commendable Chinese food. It's set on the ground floor of a stately redbrick Italianate Victorian with an attractive dining room. It's a classic menu of this genre, with so many options you wonder how the place could possibly stock all the ingredients, some of them rather unusual, on a regular basis. It's one of the best places in town for dim sum (most items are just $5–6), and the kitchen also turns out a very nice steamed half chicken with ginger and scallions. For something truly memorable (and pricey), consider the sliced Australia abalone with vegetables, or the braised sea cucumber with oyster sauce.

Quick Bites

For a memorable breakfast or lunch, don't miss

PROVIDENCE

Nick's (500 Broadway, 401/421-0286, www.nicksonbroadway.com, breakfast and lunch 7 A.M.–3 P.M. Wed.–Sat., 8 A.M.–3 P.M. Sun., dinner 5:30–10 P.M. Wed.–Sat., breakfast and lunch $6–10, dinner $15–27), a tiny oasis of amazingly delicious cooking in the city's up-and-coming West Broadway section. It's basically a hole-in-the-wall, although it's bright and airy with massive plate-glass windows, helmed by one of the city's rising culinary stars, Derek Wagner. A typically tantalizing treat is the grilled sea scallops and shrimp with citrus, apples, frisée, and honey. You can create your own omelet at breakfast (choosing from memorable ingredients such as chèvre, capers, roasted red peppers, and caramelized onions), or perhaps dig into the buttermilk hotcakes with apple-cinnamon compote along with a side of smoked salmon.

In the Jewelry District, **Olga's Cup and Saucer** (103 Point St., 401/831-6666, http://olgascupandsaucer.blogspot.com, 7 A.M.–4 P.M. Mon.–Fri., 9 A.M.–2 P.M. Sat.–Sun., baked goods $2–6, lunch $8–10) produces delicious artisanal breads, apple-hazelnut pies, lemon-blueberry pudding, chocolate-almond marble cake, and coconut oat-crisp cookies. It's a cozy nook to enjoy a pastry, bagels, and coffee breakfast or break with friends.

Haven Bros. Diner (Kennedy Plaza, 401/861-7777, 5 P.M.–3 A.M. daily, $2–5) is another of the favorite late-night greasy spoons in town, famous for its hearty breakfast food. This loveably gruff hangout is actually a diner on wheels, which the owners park outside City Hall into the wee hours.

When you're jonesing for a solid sandwich—nothing more, nothing less—head straight to **Alibi CafeRue** (18 Bassett St., 401/273-2233, 11:30 A.M.–8:30 P.M. Mon.–Sat., closed Sun., $7–9) for first-rate lunches. It serves up clever world-beat takes on the standards: The "sea quest" is a delicious dill-laden tuna fish number, and the roast beef with Boursin is a long-time favorite of regulars.

Cookie Place Cafe (280 Washington St., 401/351-8789, www.cookieplace.org/cafe, 7 A.M.–11:30 P.M. Mon.–Fri., $2–5) serves a nice variety of sandwiches (the Cajun seafood salad and bacon cheeseburger are popular options), but it's best known for its addictive chocolate-chip cookies and other baked goodies such as Heath bar toffee crunch brownies and cinnamon rolls. And if chocolate isn't your thing, the lemon-butterscotch cookies are delicious. Cookie Place is a not-for-profit organization that offers supportive employment for people with psychiatric illnesses; it's closed weekends.

Since 1929, downtown office workers have relied on **Murphy's Delicatessen** (100 Fountain St., 401/621-8467, http://murphysdeliandbar.com, 11 A.M.–1 A.M. Mon.–Thurs., 11 A.M.–2 A.M. Fri., 8 A.M.–2 A.M. Sat., 9 A.M.–1 A.M. Sun., $4–15) for filling sandwiches. Favorites include the lobster salad roll; the artery-clogging corned beef, pastrami, salami, and Swiss; and Murphy's Reuben with Irish corned beef. Several burgers are offered as well as some veggie options.

Java Joints
A hot address in the cool Downcity area, **Tazza Caffe and Lounge** (250 Westminster St., 401/421-3300, www.tazzacaffe.com, 7 A.M.–11 P.M. Mon., 7 A.M.–midnight Tues., 7 A.M.–1 A.M. Wed.–Thurs., 7 A.M.–2 A.M. Fri., 8 A.M.–2 A.M. Sat., 8 A.M.–midnight Sun., $8–16) offers all kinds of live music and readings and serves coffee and wine. The food in this hip, arty space is great too—there are sandwiches, salads, and delicious desserts. It's one of the best spots for people-watching in the city, and valet parking is available.

Gourmet Goods and Picnic Supplies
Geoff's Superlative Sandwiches (217 Westminster St., 401/273-8885) sells a wonderful array of snacks, sandwiches, and gourmet prepared foods to eat in or take out. There are signature secret sauces in almost every sandwich—witness the "Providence Monthly" (grilled chicken, melted Muenster, avocado, and Shedd's sauce on a bun), or the "Celina" (hot turkey, coleslaw, melted Havarti, and *picante* sauce).

FEDERAL HILL
Italian

On Federal Hill, Providence has one of the most prominent Little Italy neighborhoods in the country. You could easily spend a week or so sampling the specialties of every delightful grocery, trattoria, pizza place, and food shop in the district.

An upscale favorite is the **Blue Grotto** (210 Atwells Ave., 401/272-9030, 11:30 A.M.–2 P.M. Mon.–Fri., noon–3 P.M. Sat., 5–10 P.M. Mon.–Thurs., 5–10:30 P.M, Fri., 4:30–10:30 P.M. Sat.; noon–9 P.M, Sun., $15–28), a dignified restaurant whose polite, tux-clad waiters glide about the somewhat formal dining room serving plates of gnocchi with a light basil-tomato sauce and fresh mozzarella, or lobster meat and littleneck clams in a spicy marinara over risotto.

Pane e Vino (365 Atwells Ave., 401/223-2230, www.panevino.com, 5–10 P.M. Mon.–Thurs., 5–11 P.M. Fri.–Sat., 4–9 P.M. Sun. $14–24) is upscale in feel more than in price. The high caliber of cooking is impressive, from a starter of littleneck clams with a garlic-tomato broth and cannellini beans to a main course of gnocchi with a rich port wine–wild boar sauce. Desserts here are excellent, and the wine list includes more than two dozen varieties by the glass.

Tavernlike **C Mediterraneo Caffe** (134 Atwells Ave., 401/331-7760, www.mediterraneocaffe.com, 11:30 A.M.–9 P.M. Mon.–Thurs., 11:30 A.M.–10 P.M, Fri., 11:30 A.M.–1 A.M. Sat., 5–9 P.M. Sun., $14–22) is a loud and fun place with a youngish crowd. Tall French windows overlook the street, making it a prime spot to watch the world go by (everybody gravitates toward the sidewalk seating in summer). Don't think the glitzy ambience is merely a cover for so-so food: This kitchen knows what it's doing, presenting superb regional Italian fare such as a double-cut pork chops stuffed with spinach, prosciutto, and fresh mozzarella, and both straightforward and complicated pasta dishes such as fusilli with a pink vodka sauce of plum tomatoes, onions, pancetta, and heavy cream. Late at night, the place switches gears and becomes a euro-trendy dance club with an elitist velvet-rope door policy.

On reputation alone, **Angelo's Civita Farnese** (141 Atwells Ave., 401/621 81/1, www.angelosonthehill.com, 11:30 A.M.–9 P.M. Mon.–Thurs., 11:30 A.M.–10 P.M. Fri.–Sat., noon–9 P.M Sun., $4–9) could survive on any street in Providence, but here on Federal Hill it's a star among the cheaper eateries—expect heaping portions of traditional red-sauce fare in this boisterous place with communal seating. There's not much in the way of ambience, but it's fun—and former mayor Buddy Cianci loves it.

You can't miss the notably all-pink exterior of **Zooma Trattoria** (245 Atwells Ave., 401/383-2002, http://trattoriazooma.com, 11:30 A.M.–9:30 P.M. Sun.–Thurs., 11:30 A.M.–11 P.M. Fri.–Sat., $13–20), named for lyrics from the Louis Prima song "Angelina." The art-filled restaurant with high ceilings and elegant furnishings excels at creative regional Italian fare, from fresh pastas to fine grills. Save room for the luscious pear tart. There's also a first-rate wine list heavy on both Italian and North American vintages.

Geppetto's (57 De Pasquale Ave., 401/270-3003, www.geppettospizzeria.com, 11 A.M.–close daily, $6–14) is justly famous for its superb wood-fired pizzas, plus great salads, tender calamari, and a good selection of beer and wine. The restaurant doesn't have a regular closing time, but it's usually open late, with seating right on the busy square.

Try **Andino's** (171 Atwells Ave., 401/421-3715, 11 A.M.–1 A.M. daily, $10–24) for signature dishes such as chicken Andino (boneless chicken baked with artichoke hearts, sliced pepperoni, and sweet peppers in a white wine sauce); linguine with whole clams; and veal Zingarella (veal medallions sautéed with marinara sauce, roasted red peppers, sliced onions, and white mushrooms). **Joe Marzelli's Old Canteen** (120 Atwells Ave., 401/751-5544, http://theoldcanteen.com, noon–10 P.M. Wed.–Mon., closed Tues., $9–13) is an elegant white mansion made only slightly less elegant by its pulsing pink neon sign, a dependable middle-of-the-road option with reasonably priced fare. A memorable spot for desserts, especially on a warm summer evening, is **Caffe Dolce Vita**

(59 De Pasquale Ave., 401/331-8240), a coffeehouse, pastry shop, and *gelateria* whose outdoor tables are shaded with umbrellas. Across the square, drop by **Antonelli Poultry** (62 De Pasquale Ave., 401/421-8739) for the freshest chicken around, not to mention pheasant, pigeon, rabbit, and farm-fresh eggs.

You can buy fantastic handmade ravioli in about 75 varieties at **Venda Ravioli** (275 Atwells Ave., 401/421-9105), one of the most inspired delis in any Italian neighborhood in the country; here you'll find fresh sausages, sauces, oils, vinegars, cheeses, and so on. A century-old wine and liquor shop, **Gasbarro's** (361 Atwells Ave., 401/421-4170) sells some wonderful Italian imports, including about 150 varieties of chianti and almost as many of grappa. **Tony's Colonial Food** (311 Atwells Ave., 401/621-8675) is a tempting *salumeria* with just about every kind of gourmet grocery imaginable. **Roma Gourmet** (310 Atwells Ave., 401/331-8620), across from Tony's, has imported cheese, olives, sauces, and pastas, as well as hot dishes ready for takeout. Family-owned since 1916, **Scialo Bros. Bakery** (257 Atwells Ave., 401/421-0986) fires up its brick ovens daily to produce delicious Italian bread, biscotti, cakes, and pastries.

Creative but Casual

Departures from traditional Italian fare are becoming more commonplace on the Hill: Shellfish devotees should consider **Providence Oyster Bar** (283 Atwells Ave., 401/272-8866, www.providenceoysterbar.com, 4–10 P.M. Mon.–Thurs. and Sat., noon–11 P.M. Fri., $16–28), which offers a great deal more than its name suggests—although the half dozen varieties of oyster on the half shell are always fresh. The rest of the menu offers a fairly typical array of seafood, including baked Chilean sea bass with a light citrus butter and platters of fried clams and scallops. An excellent oyster stew alone qualifies as a pretty substantial meal. The menu may suggest a bare-bones spot with butcher's paper on the tables, but in fact this chatter-filled eatery is warmly lighted with dark-wood trim and a handsome long bar.

Boisterous **Opa** (244 Atwells Ave., 401/351-8282, www.providencefederalhill.com/opa, 5 P.M.–1 A.M. Mon.–Thurs., 5 P.M.–2 A.M. Fri.–Sat., $13–23) offers a slight departure from the neighborhood's usual Italian standbys, presenting mostly Greek and Middle Eastern specialties. It's a cozy spot with just a handful of tables inside and a few more along the sidewalk. Drop by for hummus platters, mixed lamb and chicken grills, and some of the freshest and most bountiful salads in town.

Ethnic Fare

Federal Hill also has an excellent Mexican restaurant, **Don Jose's Tequilas** (351 Atwells Ave., 401/454-8951, www.donjoseteq.com, 3–10 P.M. Mon.–Wed., 11:30 A.M.–11 P.M. Thurs., 11:30 A.M.–1 A.M. Fri.–Sat., 11 A.M.–10 P.M. Sun., $14–22), with a mix of Americanized and quite authentic regional dishes. The little dining room is modest but cheerfully decorated, with small tables and black bentwood chairs; extremely friendly and helpful waitstaff deliver service with a smile along with platters of chiles rellenos stuffed with mashed potatoes and jack cheese, chicken quesadillas, swordfish burritos, and chips with a smoky chipotle salsa.

In a simple, nondescript house down the hill from Federal Hill, **Chilango's Taqueria** (447 Manton Ave., at Atwells Ave., 401/383-4877, 11 A.M.–9 P.M. Sun.–Thurs., 11 A.M.–10 P.M. Fri.–Sat., $5–10) is worth the drive for perhaps the most authentic down-home Mexican food in the state, plus a nice range of Mexican beers and tequilas. It's not fancy, but that's part of the fun.

COLLEGE HILL AND THE RIVERFRONT
Upscale

Al Forno (577 S. Main St., 410/273-9760, www.alforno.com, 5–10 P.M. Tues.–Fri., 4–10 P.M. Sat., $16–32) occupies a squat warehouse near Fox Point with two-story-tall dining room windows that offer views of the ominous power plant across the Providence River and of the Hurricane Barrier. This restaurant put the neighborhood on the culinary map in 1980, and its reputation has raised the city's reputation as a dining destination—Al Forno's list of awards is almost unbelievable when you consider that it's not in one of the nation's larger cities. Among the high praise, the *International Herald Tribune* named it the world's best restaurant for casual dining. So what's all the fuss? Chef-owners (and married couple) Johanne Killeen and George Germon have made a study of northern Italian cuisine, which they prepare using—whenever appropriate—wood-burning ovens or open-flame grilling. Classic dishes include the clam roast with fiery hot sausage, tomatoes, endives, and mashed potatoes; and angel-hair noodles in fennel broth with roasted ocean catfish and peppery aioli. Pumpkin cod cake and avocado bruschetta is one of the more innovative starters. As you might guess, reservations are not easy to get—book well ahead if you can.

Waterman Grille (4 Richmond Sq., 401/521-9229, www.watermangrille.com, dinner 5–9 P.M. Mon.–Thurs., 5–10 P.M. Fri.–Sat., 5–8 P.M. Sun., brunch 10 A.M.–3 P.M. Sun., $18–29) has a less pricey pub menu in addition to more substantial fare. A lengthy list of creative martinis keeps trendsters happy. A big plus here is the location in a lovely old building on the Seekonk River. The art-filled dining room has floor-to-ceiling windows overlooking the water, so whether you come in the daytime or the evening, it's exceedingly romantic; weekend brunch is another great time to eat here. The menu emphasizes dishes like braised veal osso buco with garlic-mushroom demi-glace and celeriac mashed potatoes, or slow-roasted boneless duck with a Grand Marnier glaze and espresso sauce, praline–sweet potato hash, and sautéed and roasted vegetables.

Hemenway's Seafood Grill and Oyster Bar (121 S. Main St., 401/351-8570, www.hemenswayrestaurant.com, 11:30 A.M.–10 P.M. Mon.–Thurs., 11:30 A.M.–11 P.M. Fri.–Sat., noon–9 P.M. Sun., $17–35) is the place to go for fresh seafood. There's little pretentious or contrived about the food here—just fresh and simply prepared fish such as scampi over linguine,

fried shrimp dinners, broiled Florida grouper, baked scrod with seafood crumbs—just about every kind of fish imaginable. It's in an immense office building, but the nicest tables overlook the river. The oyster bar draws fans of the bivalve from all over the Northeast—14 varieties are served here.

Creative but Casual

Probably the most upscale and popular of the restaurants along Thayer Street, and still relatively affordable, is **Paragon/Viva** (234 Thayer St., 401/331-6200, www.paragonandviva.com, 11 A.M.–1 A.M. Sun., 11 A.M.–2 A.M. Fri.–Sat., $8–19), which occupies an airy street-corner space with funky hanging lamps and tall French door–style windows overlooking the varied pedestrian traffic. There's a lot of sidewalk seating in warm weather, and a sophisticated lounge with parquet floors and a large semicircular bar. People come here to drink as much as to nibble on tapas. If you don't look the part at this Brown University near-campus commissary, you may feel a bit out of place. The menu emphasizes creative pastas, pizzas, sandwiches, and fairly simple grills—good bets include the sea scallops with applewood smoked bacon, shallots, pinot grigio, and diced tomatoes; the lobster ravioli; the filet mignon with garlic butter; and the swordfish sandwich with a caper dill mayo.

One of several highly fashionable hangouts that have opened around Brown's campus in recent years, **Kartabar** (284 Thayer St., 401/331-8111, www.kartabar.com, 11 A.M.–1 A.M. Sun.–Thurs., 11 A.M.–2 A.M. Fri.–Sat., $10–20) is a martini lounge that has a second branch in Mexico. You might want to use a visit here as an excuse to show off those designer threads. The kitchen serves a vast array of low-maintenance comfort foods: burgers, grills, pastas, and the like, but it's more about the scene than the food.

Parkside Rotisserie and Bar (76 S. Main St., 401/331-0003, www.parksiderotisserie.com, 11:30 A.M.–10 P.M. Mon.–Thurs., 11:30 A.M.–11 P.M. Fri., 5–11 P.M. Sat., 4–9 P.M.

Sun., $15–32) is a terrific little neighborhood restaurant just across from Jackson-Gardner Park that draws a more adult and less sceney crowd than many of the restaurants this close to Brown and RISD. The staff is accommodating and fun. Inside this warmly lighted, long and narrow dining room, tables are set with crisp white napery and fringed by small wooden chairs or plush banquettes. The food is creative without going overboard, with an emphasis on pastas and rotisserie chicken as well as some excellent seafood grills. There's a nice selection of wines and beers.

Half lounge, half restaurant, **South Street Cafe** (54 South St., 401/454-5360, 11:30 A.M.–2 A.M. Tues.–Sat., closed Sun.–Mon., $13–22) rolls out a casual and solid grill menu in a somewhat noisy dining area. Some of the most popular offerings include *taquitos* and soft tacos, a roast beef sandwich with horseradish, and a hot pastrami on rye with powerful cheese.

Yuppies and students love to crowd the trendy bar at **(Rue de L'Espoir** (99 Hope St., 401/751-8890, www.therue.com, breakfast 7:30–11 A.M. Mon.–Fri., lunch 11:30 A.M.–5 P.M. Mon.–Fri., dinner 5–9 P.M. Sun.–Thurs., 5–10:30 P.M. Fri.–Sat., brunch 8:30 A.M.–2:30 P.M. Sat., 8:30 A.M.–3 P.M. Sun., $13–22) almost as much as they delight in supping here on sublime New American, Italian, and French fare—dishes include homemade ravioli filled with spinach, mushrooms, smoked Gouda, and ricotta. The restaurant maintains a friendly, low-attitude ambience. And as it's slightly off the beaten path for visitors, it has cultivated a strong following among locals since it opened back in 1976. It's a great all-around neighborhood eatery and a smart spot for brunch.

A snug and supertrendy café with exposed brick, tall gilt-frame mirrors, and walls covered with patrons' graffiti, **Café Noir** (125 N. Main St., 401/273-9090, www.cafenoirri.com, 5–10 P.M. Sun.–Thurs., 5–11 P.M. Fri.–Sat., $12–29) tends toward the outlandish, although it employs a waitstaff that can be snippy. The food combinations and preparations here can be overwrought—even outrageous—and not always executed successfully, but usually you'll come away having enjoyed a memorable and tasty meal. Before you try any food, check out the sprightly and spunky drink list—the prickly pear margarita is a nice way to start things off. It's recommended that you order dessert first (lemon meringue tart with dried cherry compote and lemon confit is a popular option). Most patrons opt for the more expected (though unusual) starters such as five-spice duck confit spring rolls with pear jam, sautéed watercress, and duck demi-glace. A typically dazzling entrée of bacon-wrapped monkfish, sage-smoked flageolet beans, baby Russian kale, and zinfandel wine sauce appeared on a recent menu, but the kitchen is always toying around with new ideas.

Although it's less pretentious than Café Noir, **Z Bar and Grille** (244 Wickenden St., 401/831-1566, www.zbarandgrille.com, 11:30 A.M.–11 P.M. Sun.–Thurs., 11:30 A.M.–2 A.M. Fri.–Sat., $11–19) nevertheless strikes a sophisticated pose on the otherwise shabby-chic Wickenden Street restaurant row. Here you'll typically find a well-put-together crowd hobnobbing behind the long polished-wood bar or dining at tables in the loud but comfy dining room with exposed brick and air ducts. When the weather cooperates, you can escape the din on the lovely brick courtyard in back. Sup on creative pizzas, large salads, appetizers such as mushroom ravioli with shiitake mushroom and tasso cream, and entrées with a contemporary bent, such as filet mignon with garlic mashed potatoes and asparagus, or chicken, broccoli rabe, tomatoes, garlic, cannellini beans, and capers tossed over angel-hair pasta. Creative "Zangwiches" (groan) include oven-roasted turkey, cranberry sauce, and seasonal stuffing served on *lavash*.

An unassuming gem on the north side of Hope Street overlooking Lippitt Memorial Park, **Chez Pascal** (960 Hope St., 401/421-4422, www.chez-pascal.com, 5:30–9:30 P.M. Mon.–Thurs., 5:30–10:30 P.M. Fri.–Sat., $25–31) prepares stellar authentic French bistro fare: coquilles St.-Jacques; asparagus, hazelnut, and watercress salad with garlic flan and hazelnut oil; hanger steak with a shallot demi-glace; escargot in puff pastry with Roquefort; and baked goat cheese over baby spinach and sliced apples. You'll also find a first-rate vegetarian tasting menu. There's nothing gimmicky about either the ingredients or the preparation, and that's why loyalists love the place. Romantics appreciate the cute, dimly lighted dining room and unrushed pace.

Serving creative and superb contemporary American fare in a riotously loud but inviting dining room, **Mill's Tavern** (101 N. Main St., 401/272-3331, www.millstavernrestaurant.com, 5–10 P.M. Mon.–Thurs., 5–11 P.M. Fri.–Sat., 4–9 P.M. Sun., $18–29) earns tremendous acclaim. Dishes such as lobster and English pea risotto with vanilla mascarpone have helped this stately spot on increasingly trendy North Main Street develop into one of the city's top venues for celebrating a special occasion.

The former owners of Downcity Food and Cocktails opened a slick but low-key neighborhood hangout along the northern reaches of Hope Street in 2005; **Cook and Brown House** (959 Hope St., 401/273-7275, http://cookandbrown.com, dinner 5:30–9:30 P.M. Tues.–Wed. and Sun, 5:30–10 P.M. Thurs.–Sat., brunch 10 A.M.–2 P.M. Sat.–Sun., $8–25) is as enjoyable for an Angus burger with horseradish sauce and a pint of beer as for fancier fare such as spiced duck breast with a blackberry, lentils, and a port-wine reduction. Don't miss the hearty brunches, served on weekends, which are as much a hit here as they continue to be at Downcity Food. Lobster cakes and eggs with home fries star among the brunch faves.

Steaks, Seafood, Pizza, and Pub Grub

Olives (108 N. Main St., 401/751-1200, www.olivesrocks.com, 5 P.M.–1 A.M. Thurs., 5 P.M.–2 A.M. Fri.–Sat., $7–11) caters to a fashionable crowd of pre-nightclub crawlers and postwork revelers. The loud and lively tavernlike eatery with high pressed-tin ceilings and French doors opening onto North Main Street serves an eclectic menu of better-than-average

comfort foods, including pasta pomodoro, sesame-orange salmon, and gourmet burgers.

Ethnic Fare

Another of the many eateries along South Main Street, **Pakarang** (303 S. Main St., 401/453-3660, www.pakarangrestaurant.com, lunch 11:30 A.M.–3 P.M. Tues.–Fri., noon–3 P.M. Sat., dinner 5–10 P.M. Sun.–Thurs., 5–10:30 P.M. Fri.–Sat., $11–18) is a reliable option for Thai; it's a lively, cleverly decorated spot with mounted fish "swimming" against a brick sea. House specialties include Choo Choo curry with snow peas, pineapple, peppers, zucchini, summer squash, and tomato; and sliced sautéed salmon with ginger, asparagus, onion, carrot, black mushrooms, red pepper, and scallions.

O-cha (221 Wickenden St., 401/421-4699, noon–10 P.M. daily, $5–16) is a cute little Asian eatery on the ground floor of a handsome old Wickenden Victorian—it's tiny but cozy with an almost familial-seeming staff that ranges from cheerful to gruff, and there's some outdoor seating on the side deck. The menu mixes Thai recipes (spicy duck topped with Thai herbs in wine sauce, beef with coconut curry, pad thai) with traditional Japanese sushi.

On the college strip, **Kebob-n-Curry** (261 Thayer St., 401/273-8844, www.kabobandcurry.com, 11 A.M.–10:30 P.M. Mon.–Thurs., 11 A.M.–11 P.M. Fri.–Sat., 11:30 A.M.–10 P.M. Sun., $7–14) presents an ambitious menu of Indian specialties, from the usual tikka masala and vindaloo to less predictable creations such as lamb chops marinated in mint and white wine or chunks of cod baked with cumin.

Taste of India (230 Wickenden St., 401/421-4355, www.tasteofindiaprovri.com, lunch 11:30 A.M.–2:30 P.M. Mon.–Fri., noon–3 P.M. Sat.–Sun., dinner 5–10 P.M. Mon.–Sat., 5–9:30 P.M. Sun., $11–17) is one of the very best bets in town for fine Indian cooking. Soft pink walls brighten an otherwise plain dining room, but this restaurant is recommended for its exceptionally fresh and well-seasoned food. The menu runs a fairly traditional course, with the usual tandoori, meat with spiced spinach, naan and *kulcha* Indian breads, *pakora* deep-fried vegetables, and the like.

India (1060 Hope St., 401/421-2600, www.indiarestaurant.com, 11 A.M.–10 P.M. Sun.–Thurs., 11 A.M.–11 P.M. Fri.–Sat., $9–16) brings excellent Indian fare to the northeast side of town. In addition to the standbys, India offers some unusual options like *papri chat,* an Indian take on nachos, with chickpeas, onions, cilantro, yogurt, and tamarind chutney; seafood in sweet-and-sour mango and cashew sauce; and swordfish kabobs. It is one of the best eateries of this genre in the state for it's food as well as for the imaginative and bold decor, with bright paintings, hanging Oriental rugs, and elegant light fixtures.

A Thayer Street mainstay since the 1960s, casual yet snazzy **Andreas Restaurant** (268 Thayer St., 401/331-7879, www.andreasri.com, 11 A.M.–1 A.M. Mon.–Fri., 9 A.M.–2 A.M. Sat.–Sun., $7–20) is a lively, always crowded Greek restaurant with a smartly furnished dining room and big windows overlooking the street. You can grab a lamb burger or grilled calamari appetizer, or opt for something more substantial, such as flame-broiled salmon with olive oil or pastitsio casserole topped with béchamel sauce. There's also a nice wine list.

A departure from the slick contemporary interior of so many Japanese restaurants, **Sakura** (231 Wickenden St., 401/331-6861, www.eat-inri.com/sakura, 11 A.M.–11 P.M. daily, $9–15) almost feels a bit cluttered (in a good way), set inside a grand old rambling wood-frame house with creaky wide-plank floors. Sushi rolls include dragon *maki* with eel, cucumber, rice, and avocado; and a crispy *kirin maki* that's lightly fried and filled with tuna, salmon, and whitefish. Entrée favorites include barbecued beef rolled with scallions, tuna teriyaki, and several tasty *udon* and soba noodle dishes.

Up near the Pawtucket border at the north end of Blackstone Boulevard, **Ran Zan Japanese Restaurant** (1084 Hope St., 401/276-7574, www.ranzan.net, lunch 11:30 A.M.–2:30 P.M. Tues.–Fri. and Sun., dinner 5–9:30 P.M. Tues.–Thurs., 5–10 P.M.

Fri.–Sat., 5–9 P.M. Sun., $9–18) is a hole-in-the-wall with a young and accommodating staff and a low-key ambience that replicates the experience of eating over at a friend's house (assuming you have a friend who cooks very good Japanese food and prepares fresh sushi). Pork *katsu,* shrimp *yakisoba,* snow crab–asparagus rolls, and various sushi combos are offered at quite reasonable prices.

Tortilla Flats (355 Hope St., 401/751-6777, www.tortillaflatsri.com, 11:30 A.M.–1 A.M. Mon.–Thurs., 11:30 A.M.–2 A.M. Fri.–Sat., 1 P.M.–1 A.M. Sun., $8–14) serves pretty tasty Mexican food, including a house specialty called the cactus flower, a tortilla basket stuffed with lettuce, tomato, cheese, guacamole, and olives, topped with grilled steak or chicken breast. It's no better or more authentic than most Mexican restaurants in Providence, but it has a pleasant ambience and serves consistently fresh food.

Quick Bites

Geoff's (163 Benefit St., 401/751-2248, www.geoffsonline.com, 10 A.M.–9 P.M. daily, $4–6), your source for hefty sandwiches along Thayer Street, suffers from indifferent service and a dull little dining room. But you eat here for the amazing sandwiches: try the Chicken George, with chicken salad, bacon, melted Swiss, hot spinach, tomato, onion, and Russian dressing; or the Mike Schwartz, with tuna, hot pastrami, Muenster, Russian dressing, lettuce, and tomato. More prosaic varieties are also offered, but it's the massive and elaborate creations that have earned Geoff's its sterling reputation.

La Creperie (82 Fones Alley, 401/751-5536, www.creperieprov.com, 10 A.M.–midnight Mon.–Thurs., 10 A.M.–2 A.M. Fri., 9 A.M.–2 A.M. Sat., 9 A.M.–midnight Sun., $3–6) is a tiny spot down an alley off Thayer Street, but this homey little place serves very good sweet and savory crepes, and it stays open very late (one wonders how, as so few people walk by it). Fresh fruit smoothies are another house specialty.

Of all the quasi-fast-food eateries along Thayer Street, **Spike's Junkyard Dogs** (485

COURTESY OF PROVIDENCE WARWICK CVB

The Coffee Exchange on Wickenden Street

Branch Ave., 401/861-6888, www.spikesjunk-yarddogs.com, 11 A.M.–11 P.M. Mon.–Thurs., 11 A.M.–1:30 A.M. Fri.–Sat., noon–10 P.M. Sun., $2–6) most deserves the chance to harden your arteries—the dogs here are exquisite, especially the chili-and-cheddar dog. They also serve subs.

Just off Thayer Street, the **Meeting Street Cafe** (220 Meeting St., 401/273-1066, www.meetingstreetcafe.com, 8 A.M.–11 P.M. daily, $3–7) serves immensely satisfying scones, pastries, pies, cookies, and light breakfast and lunch fare.

A hit with students from nearby RISD and Brown, **Cable Car Cinema** (204 S. Main St., 401/272-3970, www.cablecarcinema.com, 8 A.M.–11 P.M. Mon.–Fri., 9 A.M.–11 P.M. Sat.–Sun., $4–8) is known as much for its cheap and cheerful dining as for its art-film theater. White-tuna and other sandwiches, homemade soups, bagels and spreads, fresh-baked cookies, coffees, and all sorts of sweets are served in this quaint café with the black-and-white-striped awning.

Sun-filled **Brickway** (234 Wickenden St., 401/751-2477, 7 A.M.–3 P.M. Mon.–Fri., 8 A.M.–3 P.M. Sat.–Sun., $4–8), which has an inviting little brick terrace, is a casual spot with outstanding breakfasts and lunches in heart of Wickenden's dining area. About 10 kinds of pancakes and French toast are offered, including chocolate-chip and Caribbean, with pineapple, banana, and kiwi, plus great omelets and other egg dishes. Lunch options include curried chicken and pasta salad, veggie burgers and hamburgers, and hot and cold sandwiches.

Up at the northern end of Blackstone Boulevard and lovely Lippitt Memorial Park, ◖ **Three Sisters** (1074 Hope St., 401/273-7230, www.threesistersri.com, 6:30 A.M.–9 P.M. Mon.–Thurs., 6:30 A.M.–10 P.M. Fri., 8 A.M.–10 P.M. Sat., 8 A.M.–9 P.M. Sun., $3–7) is a good spot for snacking. This dark and cozy little parlor has frozen treats of many, many flavors, plus wraps, BLTs, soups, and other savories.

Java Joints

The Coffee Exchange (207 Wickenden St., 401/273-1198, www.sustainablecoffee.com, 6:30 A.M.–11 P.M. daily, under $4) occupies an attractive Second Empire Victorian house on Wickenden Street filled with bric-a-brac and coffee-related goods. There's also an attractive patio. The coffeehouse donates a share of its take to needy workers, many of them children, who struggle to make a scant living employed on coffee farms in poor countries.

Cafe Zog (239 Wickenden St., 401/421-2213, 7:30 A.M.–11 P.M. daily, $3–6) serves healthful salads, prepared foods, and *chai* teas to patrons tucked in around closely spaced tables and watching the world stroll by on Wickenden Street. Zog offers what might be one of the best bargains in the city: A few bucks gets you an omelet with your choice of numerous fillings and a nice bagel with cream cheese or butter.

Gourmet Goods and Picnic Supplies

For years, indigent college students have been

PROVIDENCE

spending what little money they have on the delectable baked goods at **729 Hope Street** (729 Hope St., 401/273-7290), a bakery and gourmet food shop. White-chocolate Cage Cake is the house specialty, and coffees and sandwiches are available.

A fabulous café and bakery with floor-to-ceiling windows and a sunny patio out on the side, **((** **Seven Stars** (820 Hope St., 401/521-2200, www.sevenstarsbakery.com, 6:30 A.M.–6 P.M. Mon.–Fri., 7 A.M.–6 P.M. Sat.–Sun., $2–7) serves delicious ginger biscuits, individual-size lemon cakes, olive bread, gooey chocolate brownies, and ham-and-cheese calzones, and it has a delightful garden patio that's great for sipping espresso.

In Fox Point, fans of Portuguese cooking shouldn't miss either the **Taunton Ave. Bakery** (208 Taunton Ave., 401/434-3450, 5 A.M.–7:30 P.M. Mon.–Fri., 5 A.M.–7 P.M. Sun.), famous for its Portuguese sweet bread, or the **Friends Market** (126 Brook St., 401/861-0345, 9 A.M.–5:30 P.M. daily), which carries imported delicacies from the mother country.

OLNEYVILLE AND ENVIRONS

Well west of downtown in the Olneyville neighborhood, **Wes's Rib House** (38 Dike St., 401/421-9090, www.wesribhouse. com, 11:30 A.M.–2 A.M. Mon.–Thurs., 11:30 A.M.–4 A.M. Fri.–Sat., noon–2 A.M. Sun., $6–16) is a down-home Missouri-style barbecue spot that's worth the trip. Savor the Show Me platter (comes with your choice of four meats plus coleslaw, barbecue beans, and cornbread), or try the individual ribs, chicken, beef, and other plates. Well south of downtown, the **Portuguese American Market** (896 Allens Ave., 401/941-4480, 8 A.M.–5 P.M. daily) is the place to stock up on fava beans, linguica, salt cod, and fresh-baked sweetbreads.

Information and Services

VISITOR INFORMATION

For maps, updates on the city's events, and any other visitor information, call or stop by the **Providence Warwick Convention and Visitors Bureau** (1 W. Exchange St., 401/274-1636, www.pwcvb.com). You can also stop by the **Providence Visitors Center** (1 Sabin St., 401/751-1177), another vast repository of brochures and information, located inside the Rhode Island Convention Center.

Some major hospitals include: **Kent Hospital** (455 Toll Gate Rd., Warwick, 401/737-7000 or 888/455-KENT—888/455-5368, www. kentri.org), **Memorial Hospital of Rhode Island** (111 Brewster St., Pawtucket, 401/729-2000, www.mhri.org), **Mirium Hospital** (164 Summit Ave., Providence, 401/793-2500, www.lifespan.org/partners), **Rhode Island Hospital** (593 Eddy St., Providence, 401/444-4000, www.lifespan.org/partners/rih), **Our Lady of Fatima Hospital** (200 High Service Ave., North Providence, 401/456-3000), **St. Joseph Hospital for Specialty Care** (Peace St., Providence, 401/456-3000, www.saint-josephri.com), **South County Hospital** (100 Kenyon Ave., Wakefield, 401/782-8000, www. schospital.com), and **Westerly Hospital** (Wells St., Westerly, 401/596-6000, www.westerly-hospital.com).

You'll find pharmacies, many of them open until 9 or 10 P.M., throughout the city; the leading chain is CVS (www.cvs.com). Pharmacies open 24 hours include **East Providence CVS** (640 Warren Ave., East Providence, 401/438-2272) and **North Providence CVS** (1919 Mineral Spring Ave., North Providence, 401/353-2501).

Banks are found all over the downtown area, in the college neighborhoods, and in areas frequented by tourists, and ATMs are scattered throughout the city.

Internet is available for free in libraries and

for a small fee (usually a few dollars per hour) in cafés and at **FedEx Office** (100 Westminster St., 401/331-1990), which also provides faxing and shipping services. Free Wi-Fi is offered at **Coffee Connection** (207 Wickenden St.), Cuban Revolution (50 Aborn St.), and other locations around town.

MEDIA

The city's (and the region's) daily newspaper is the *Providence Journal* (401/277-7700, www.projo.com). The paper has an outstanding and highly informative website with information on local dining, arts, music, travel, and kids-oriented activities, and it has recently been recognized for its breaking news coverage online. An excellent resource for metro Providence arts, dining, shopping, clubbing, and similar such diversions is the decidedly left-of-center *Providence Phoenix* alternative newsweekly (401/273-6397, www.thephoenix.com). Also look to the lively and free *Providence Monthly* (www.providenceonline.com, 401/521-0023), a glossy magazine, for great features on the city along with first-rate dining, shopping, and nightlife coverage.

Grab the free monthly *Federal Hill Gazette* (401/521-2701) for the scoop on one of the city's liveliest neighborhoods.

Other area papers include the twice-weekly *Warwick Beacon* (401/732-3100, www.warwickonline.com) and the *Kent County Daily Times* (401/821-7400, www.ricentral.com). **Southern Rhode Island Newspapers** (401/789-9744, www.ricentral.com) publishes several local weeklies, including *The Chariho Times* (Wyoming), *The Coventry Courier, The East Greenwich Pendulum,* and *The Standard Times.*

TOURS

Providence River Boat Co. (575 S. Water St., 401/580-BOAT—401/580-2628) offers water-taxi service, sightseeing cruises, and charter tours of the Providence waterfront and out into Narragansett Bay. **Conway Tours/Gray Line Rhode Island** (10 Nate Whipple Hwy., Cumberland, 401/658-3400 or 800/888-4661, www.conwaytours.com) runs all kinds of bus and boat tours of the region, including daily trips to Connecticut's Foxwoods Casino from Providence and cruises on Providence harbor.

Getting There and Around

GETTING THERE
By Air

Providence's international airport **T. F. Green Airport** (2000 Post Rd., Warwick, 888/268-7222 or 401/691-2471, www.pvdairport.com) is located south of the city and has regular flights from many U.S. and Canadian cities by Air Canada, Delta, US Airways, and other carriers.

By Bus

The **Rhode Island Public Transit Authority (RIPTA)** (401/781-9400 or 800/244-0444, www.ripta.com) runs frequent buses from T. F. Green to downtown for a fare of $1.75 one-way. In addition, **Peter Pan Bus Lines** (800/343-9999, www.peterpanbus.com) runs buses to Providence from throughout New

England, stopping at 1 Peter Pan Way (north of town, off exit 25 from I-95) and downtown (1 Kennedy Plaza). **Greyhound** (800/231-2222, www.greyhound.com) also connects to Providence from many U.S. cities, also stopping at 1 Kennedy Plaza.

By Train

It's fairly easy to get to Providence by train aboard **Amtrak** (800/872-7245, www.amtrak.com). Trains stop in Providence on their way from Washington D.C. (6 hours), New York (3.5 hours), and Boston (40 minutes).

GETTING AROUND
Buses

Bus travel is inexpensive and relatively

convenient throughout the state on the **Rhode Island Transportation Authority (RIPTA) buses** (401/781-9400, www.ripta.com). Kennedy Plaza, in the heart of downtown, is the nexus for bus routes all over Rhode Island. Fares start at just $1.75 for any ride within a mile of downtown (transfers are an additional $0.50). Have some coins with you, as exact change is required. There are student discounts as well as monthly passes. Buses generally run 5:30 A.M.– midnight, and the Providence Visitors Center and the Convention and Visitors Bureau distribute free maps that detail popular routes.

In addition, both locals and visitors have taken a shine to the city's pleasant and inexpensive **LINK trolley.** The Green Line runs from Fox Point up through College Hill, past Thayer Street, and then west across downtown and over to colorful Federal Hill. The Gold line runs from the State House south through downtown and the Jewelry District, with a stop at the Providence ferry landing, terminating in the Southside at Blackstone. The fare is $1.75 for any ride on the system, and monthly and 10-ride discount passes are offered. LINK trolleys make their appointed stops every 20 minutes, on the Green Line 6:30 A.M.–9 P.M. Monday–Friday, 8 A.M.–6:30 P.M. Saturday, 11 A.M.–6:30 P.M. Sunday, and on the Gold Line 6:30 A.M.–7 P.M. Monday–Friday, 8:30 A.M.–6:30 P.M. Saturday, 11 A.M.–6:30 P.M. Sunday.

Driving and Parking

The pace of driving in Providence is less chaotic than in Boston, but this is still a Type A kind of place: People drive fast and use their horns. One-way, narrow, and crooked streets proliferate and can be confusing and frustrating (although they are charming to walk). Overall, if you're fairly used to driving and parking in urban environments, Providence is reasonably navigable.

Parking garages abound downtown but can be rather expensive. A smart strategy is to park at the 5,000-space, nine-level Providence Place Mall, which is within easy walking distance of most downtown attractions and is extremely economical, but only if you get your parking ticket validated at a shop in the mall. You don't have to buy anything pricey to get the validation—any store or eatery there can stamp your ticket.

Providence is a relatively safe city, and you don't often hear of car theft or break-ins, but it certainly can and does happen. You'll save a lot of money opting for street parking over garage or supervised-lot parking, but you also open yourself up to the risk of theft.

Taxis

People don't generally hail cabs on the street in Providence, but you can find them at major hotels and occasionally outside clubs at night. For trips to the airport or coming home late from a bar or restaurant, call ahead to **AA 24 Hour Taxi** (401/521-4200) and **American Cab** (401/487-2111). The fare is $2.50 per mile.

OUTSIDE PROVIDENCE

It's an old joke in Rhode Island, since the state is so small, that everyone except those who live in the capital can simply describe their residence as "outside Providence." There is, however, a distinct corner of the northwestern part of the state that is more aptly called Greater Providence as opposed to, say, the East Bay or South County. While it may not have a cohesive identity as such, the roughly square section of Rhode Island that encompasses some dozen towns and cities accounts for nearly half the area of the state. Within those boundaries are both some of the state's largest cities and its quietest townships. And while there may not be as many formal attractions as in other parts of the state, there are still several top-flight museums and a bevy of recreational opportunities in wild landscapes of forest, river, and wetlands.

The most appealing part of this region for visitors is the area directly north of Providence known as the Blackstone River Valley. This small corner of the smallest state has had an outsized influence on the history of the nation as a whole. It was here in the early 1800s in cities like Pawtucket and Woonsocket that industrious entrepreneurs began harnessing the power of the Blackstone River to create the nation's first textile mills. The factories were so successful at reducing labor and generating wealth that they were soon replicated throughout the Northeast, spurring the American industrial revolution that established the United States as a true world power within a generation. Much of this industrial history has been preserved in several museums as well as old mill buildings throughout the region that have

COURTESY OF PROVIDENCE WARWICK CVB

OUTSIDE PROVIDENCE

HIGHLIGHTS

LOOK FOR ◖ TO FIND RECOMMENDED SIGHTS, ACTIVITIES, DINING, AND LODGING.

◖ **Slater Mill:** This beautifully preserved complex contains important late-colonial factory buildings and machinery that figured prominently in the American industrial revolution (page 61).

◖ **Slater Park:** A crazy quilt of ball fields, picnic sites, and historic sites, anchored by the famous 1895 Looff Carousel (page 64).

◖ **Museum of Work and Culture:** In the otherwise prosaic little city of Woonsocket, a 20-minute drive northwest of Providence, this museum run by the Rhode Island Historical Society illuminates the ordinary and extraordinary lives of the thousands of mostly immigrant mill and factory workers who made the state what it is today (page 67).

◖ **PawSox:** A favorite Rhode Island tradition is a night at the ball game, where the Red Sox's future stars are born (page 72).

◖ **Kayaking the Blackstone:** Not your ordinary kayaking experience, the rushing Blackstone offers a different view on Rhode Island's industrial past (page 72).

been converted into condos, offices, and art studios.

To the west, the river valley merges with Rhode Island's "quiet corner," a half-dozen towns that have resisted development of any kind to remain a bucolic vision of what New England looked like 100 years ago. You won't find any megamalls or amusement parks here—in fact, you won't find many hotels or restaurants either. But you will find miles of backcountry roads lined with stone walls, orchards, farm stands, and historic homes. This area comes alive especially during foliage season, when colorful red maples and yellow beeches frame postcard-ready small-town tableaux.

By contrast, the coastal area south of Providence along Narragansett Bay is home to the urbanization of Rhode Island's two largest cities after Providence—Cranston and

Warwick. Unlike the capital, they have decidedly not gone through a renaissance. They remain gritty, working-class cities that offer a glimpse of the real lives of many Rhode Islanders without pretense. While there are no formal attractions for visitors in either city, Warwick has some pretty neighborhoods on the bay worth driving through, as well as some pretty beaches that are the closest place to Providence to sunbathe or take a dip.

PLANNING YOUR TIME

Truth be told, the Outside Providence area is better-suited to day trips than overnight stays. After your second or third day in Providence, it is almost mandatory to take a drive north to see the industrial towns of Pawtucket and Woonsocket. You can visit both towns in an afternoon, but it's more enjoyable to make an entire day of it, taking time at the historic sites,

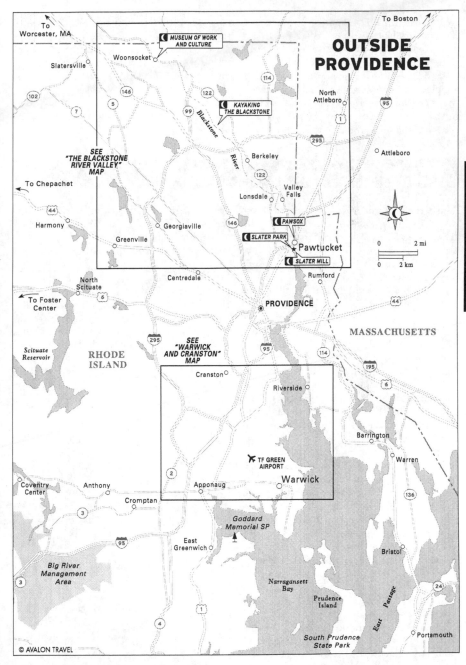

To Worcester, MA

To Boston

MUSEUM OF WORK AND CULTURE

Woonsocket

Slatersville

OUTSIDE PROVIDENCE

114

102

146

122

North Attleboro

95

7

5

99

KAYAKING THE BLACKSTONE

1

Blackstone

295

SEE "THE BLACKSTONE RIVER VALLEY" MAP

Berkeley

River

Attleboro

To Chepachet

44

122

Valley Falls

Harmony

146

Lonsdale

PAWSOX

Georgiaville

0   2 mi

Greenville

SLATER PARK

Pawtucket

0   2 km

SLATER MILL

North Scituate

Centredale

Rumford

To Foster Center

6

PROVIDENCE

44

MASSACHUSETTS

Scituate Reservoir

295

SEE "WARWICK AND CRANSTON" MAP

95

114

RHODE ISLAND

195

6

Cranston

Riverside

Barrington

Warren

TF GREEN AIRPORT

Coventry Center

Anthony

Apponaug

Warwick

136

3

Cromptan

95

Big River Management Area

East Greenwich

Goddard Memorial SP

Bristol

3

Narragansett Bay

Prudence Island

East Passage

24

1

4

South Prudence State Park

Portsmouth

© AVALON TRAVEL

stopping at an ethnic restaurant for lunch, picnicking in Slater Park, or taking in a night game by the PawSox—the Boston Red Sox's minor league team.

If the outdoors are more your thing, there are plenty of opportunities for hiking, kayaking, and canoeing along the river as well as in the natural preserves in the far northwest corner of the state. You can take as little or as long as you want to view the bucolic towns of the "quiet corner"—although during foliage season, you could plan at least half a day to drive the back roads, perhaps passing through on your way to South County. Alternately, pass through Cranston and Warwick on your way south for a drive around historic neighborhoods or for clam cakes and people-watching on the waterfront.

The Blackstone River Valley

The part of Greater Providence with the most distinct cultural and historic identity is the Blackstone River Valley, which begins just north of Providence in Pawtucket and extends north to Woonsocket, encompassing a swath of nearby communities. In this area you can get a sense of how the nation shifted from being an agrarian land of farmers, independent artisans, and skilled craftspeople to a full-fledged industrial powerhouse. Shortly after the War of Independence, complete mill communities—with worker housing, community halls and churches, and massive mill buildings—sprang up all along the Blackstone River and its tributaries, from Pawtucket north through Woonsocket and across the Massachusetts border to Worcester, nearly 50 miles away.

In the course of its 46 miles the Blackstone River plummets about 450 feet—a rate of 10 feet per mile, more than the Colorado River drops as it passes through the Grand Canyon. As early as 1665, settlers began damming sections of the river, harnessing the energy of the powerful flow to run mills. By the late 19th century, the once crystal-clear Blackstone had become one of the hardest-working, most heavily dammed, and most polluted rivers in North America. In 1986 Congress designated the river as the John H. Chafee Blackstone River Valley National Heritage Corridor, and since that time major efforts have been made to clean it up and preserve both its pristine and industrial elements. Although Pawtucket and Woonsocket are bustling, if rather small, cities, the Blackstone River Valley nevertheless has a surprising number of areas with low population density and an almost rural character.

PAWTUCKET

Pawtucket (population 72,000) is a classic river town, its eastern and western boundaries formed by the Ten Mile and Moshassuck Rivers. The river for which it's most famous, however, is the Blackstone, which cuts through

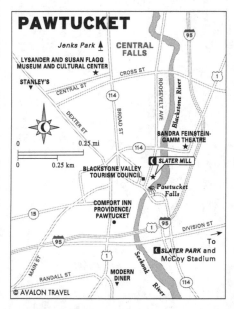

the center of the city. In colonial times the Blackstone River was the border between Rhode Island and Massachusetts. In 1874 the communities on both sides of the river formed one community that incorporated in 1885 as the city of Pawtucket. Since then, it has remained a densely packed little downtown of crooked and narrow side streets mostly emanating from the main drags, Main and Broad Streets and East Avenue.

The city has always had a hard-nosed, working-class personality, but at the same time it's without much urban blight and decay. Modest double-decker and triple-decker tenement housing proliferates in many neighborhoods, and large numbers of Italians, Portuguese, Puerto Ricans, and African Americans—along with smaller factions of myriad other ethnicities— make up the population. More recently, young professionals have moved in to take advantage of cheap real estate and proximity to Boston; it's only a matter of time before it blossoms with more sophisticated dining, shopping, and nightlife options.

(Slater Mill

For all intents and purposes, the American industrial revolution started at Slater Mill (Main St. and Roosevelt Ave., 401/725-8638, www.slatermill.org, 11 A.M.–3 P.M. Sat.–Sun. Mar.–Apr., 10 A.M.–4 P.M. Tues.–Sun. May–Oct., group tours by appointment Nov.–Feb., $12 adults, $8.50 children), a collection of mill buildings now preserved as a historic site along the Blackstone River. Young English immigrant Samuel Slater took a job in Ezekiel Carpenter's clothing shop, and by recalling the exact blueprints for water-powered textile machinery in his native country, developed the nation's first such textile factory. A 10,000-square-foot visitors center across from the mill provides orientation with an 18-minute video offering a stark view of mill life in Rhode Island.

The 5.5-acre site has several buildings, including the three-story **Wilkenson House,** built in 1810 on the site of an old metal works, which contains a full machine shop on the ground floor and a re-creation of the mill's massive waterwheel in the basement. During

OUTSIDE PROVIDENCE

COURTESY OF SLATER MILL

the machine shop at Slater Mill

the tour, you watch a nine-ton wooden water-wheel turn and spread the power through the building, the gears turning a series of pulleys that in turn power individual tools and machines. About 20 woodworkers and metalworkers worked in the Wilkenson House's first-floor machine shop. During the tour a guide demonstrates exactly how a drill is powered by the millrace.

Perhaps the most striking of the site's structures, the **Old Slater Mill** is a sturdy 1793 wooden structure commissioned by William Almy, Obadiah Brown, and Samuel Slater and built by local Pawtucket laborers. Sunlight streams through the building's many soaring windows. Within just a few months of its construction, the factory had turned out the first cotton yarn produced in the New World. Inside, you'll find a few original machines from the period and many more authentic replicas that provide a clear sense of how these factories operated in the early days. Many of the machines were either designed or modified by Samuel Slater himself. At one end of the building a small museum store sells penny candy and small gifts, including work by local artisans and fiber artists as well as a selection of books on industrial history and textile crafts.

Moved here in 1962, having been spared destruction when I-95 was built through Pawtucket, the 1758 **Sylvanus Brown** house, a nicely restored gambrel-roof colonial, is also part of the tour. Demonstrations of flax-weaving are often given inside—a garden of flax was installed behind the house in 2000. (The golden-colored debris left after flax has been combed through a large metal hackle is called tow, hence the term *towheaded* to describe a blond-haired child.) Millwright Sylvanus Brown ran the house as a carpenter's shop during the late 1700s. It has been fully restored to its original appearance.

The massive dam that runs across the Blackstone River from the Old Slater Mill dates to 1792. Running from above the dam and under the Old Slater Mill to the front of Wilkinson Mill, **Slater's Trench** (also known as the Great Flume) siphoned water from the

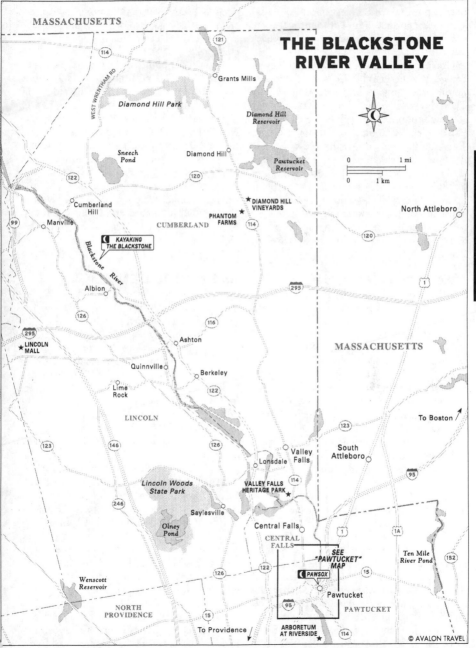

THE BLACKSTONE RIVER VALLEY

MASSACHUSETTS

Grants Mills

Diamond Hill Park

Diamond Hill Reservoir

Sneech Pond

Diamond Hill

Pawtucket Reservoir

WEST WRENTHAM RD

★ DIAMOND HILL VINEYARDS

North Attleboro

Cumberland Hill

CUMBERLAND

PHANTOM FARMS

Manville

KAYAKING THE BLACKSTONE

Blackstone River

Albion

★ LINCOLN MALL

Ashton

MASSACHUSETTS

Quinnville

Berkeley

Lime Rock

LINCOLN

To Boston ↗

Valley Falls

South Attleboro

Lonsdale

Lincoln Woods State Park

VALLEY FALLS HERITAGE PARK ★

Saylesville

Central Falls

Olney Pond

CENTRAL FALLS

SEE "PAWTUCKET" MAP

Ten Mile River Pond

Wenscott Reservoir

PAWSOX

NORTH PROVIDENCE

Pawtucket

PAWTUCKET

To Providence ↓

ARBORETUM AT RIVERSIDE ★

0   1 mi
0   1 km

© AVALON TRAVEL

river to power the machinery of the two mills. The water continued into **Sargeant's Trench,** which sent the water below the falls and back into the river.

Crashing down below the Main Street Bridge, Pawtucket Falls were a natural formation improved by artificial damming in 1718. These days the falls are faced in brick, and they continue to provide power to the Blackstone Valley Electric Company just downstream. The double-arch, cut-stone **Main Street Bridge,** from which you can get great views of the entire Slater Mill Historic Site, dates to 1858, but a bridge has stood at this point since 1714. Ezekiel Carpenter's original clothing shop stood on the southwest corner of the Main Street bridge and the river; it's where Samuel Slater first worked when he arrived in Pawtucket.

Arboretum at Riverside

Another noteworthy sight in Pawtucket is the Arboretum at Riverside (724 Pleasant St., 10 A.M.–2 P.M. Tues.–Sun., $5), where you can explore 80 acres of beautifully landscaped pathways and gardens along the Seekonk River, into which the Blackstone flows below Pawtucket Falls. Among the varieties of trees you're apt to find while strolling here are black oak, eastern red cedar, ginkgo, wild black cherry, big-tooth aspen, and white ash. Shrubs from as far away as Japan and central Asia thrive here, plus impressive stands of azaleas and rhododendrons. The arboretum is tended organically, using only natural fertilizers and pesticides.

◖ Slater Park

In the northeastern section of town, near the Massachusetts border, lies Slater Park (401/728-0500, ext. 252), which has entrances on both Newport Avenue (Rte. 1A) and Armistice Boulevard (Rte. 15). There are 18 picnic sites plus tennis courts, ball fields, gardens, and other diversions to while away a pleasant afternoon. Chief among them is a **Looff Carousel** (401/728-0500, ext. 316, 11 A.M.–5 P.M. Sat.–Sun. Apr.–June and Sept.–Oct., 11 A.M.–5 P.M. daily July–Aug., $0.25), which dates to 1895.

Charles I. D. Looff ranks among the earliest and most distinguished designers of carousels, and Slater Park's ride contains 50 whimsical characters.

The park is home to the historic **Daggett House** (401/722-6931, group tours 2–5 P.M. Sat.–Sun. June–Sept., $2 pp), the oldest extant house in the city, furnished in the period style with fine antiques, vintage pewter, and Revolutionary War–era china. Eight generations of Daggetts lived in the house through the years. The house is only open for groups of 15–20 people, but you can still admire the exterior.

Art aficionados might want to check out the **Rhode Island Watercolor Society Gallery** (in the park's J. C. Potter Casino, 401/726-1876, www.riws.org, 10 A.M.–4 P.M. Tues.–Sat., 1–5 P.M. Sun., free).

EAST PROVIDENCE

From downtown Pawtucket, drive south four miles along Route 114 to the center of this semi-industrial suburb just over the I-195 bridge from Providence. The town is often thought of as little more than an extension of Providence, a reputation it has had since it was founded in 1862. In reality East Providence has become a small industrial city like Pawtucket, its neighbor to the north, producing baking powder, refining petroleum, and engaging in other light industry. The city contains a few notable sites, especially toward the north part of town.

From Route 114, bear left onto Route 114A and make a right turn onto Hunt Mills Road. Just a few yards from the Massachusetts border, the **East Providence Historical Society** (Hunt Mills Rd., Rumford, 401/438-1750, http://ephist.org, 1–4 P.M. the second Sun. of every month, $3) makes its home in the Georgian-style John Hunt House in the historic Hunt Mills neighborhood of Rumford, a village within East Providence. The five-bay, center-chimney colonial was constructed in 1750 and then added to significantly in 1790. Inside, it is furnished as an upper-class country house of the day would have been; you'll find a varied collection of memorabilia, tools, documents, and photographs, most of them donated by residents through the years, that paint a picture of East Providence's history. Every couple of years changing exhibits are installed.

The historical society also manages the **Philip Walker House** (432 Massasoit Ave.), the oldest extant house in the city and the second oldest in Rhode Island, dating to 1676. A typical three-bay house with a central chimney, the structure was burned during King Philip's War but was rebuilt three years later. It remains an excellent example of very early colonial architecture and is worth a drive-by for anyone interested in the period. It is not currently open to visitors, but some furniture and other artifacts from the house are displayed in a special room in the society's Hunt House headquarters.

South from downtown East Providence along the waterfront is Crescent Park (take Rte. 103 S. and bear right onto Bullocks Point Ave.). Kids and any adult with fond childhood memories of carousels will get a kick out of the **Charles I. D. Looff Carousel** (700 Bullocks Point Ave., 401/435-7518, $1). This wooden 1895 structure has long been recognized as one of Looff's most beautiful and ornate designs. On it there are 62 figures carved of wood and four chariots. Beveled mirrors, faceted glass, and twinkling lights add further sparkle to the clanging contraption that rotates to the sounds of Wurlitzer organ music. The hours vary through the year, but you should be able to ride noon–7 P.M. on weekends from about Easter through Columbus Day. Call if you're visiting on a weekday, as it's sometimes open all week in summer. There's a small food concession where you can snack on clam cakes, chowder, and other traditional short-order favorites.

Central Falls

Little Central Falls lies just a mile north of downtown Pawtucket along Route 114. It's just a mile square, making it the smallest community in the nation's smallest state. The town began its foray into industrialization

with the foundation of a chocolate factory in 1790; for many years this area was called simply Chocolate Mill. Later, in the 19th century, gold and silver electrolytic extraction as well as textile businesses appeared. In the center of the village, a couple of blocks north of Central Street, is four-acre **Jenks Park** (Broad St., Rte. 114, 401/727-7480), home of the four-faced 1904 Cogswell Clock Tower atop Dexter's Ledge, which the Indians used as a watchtower during King Philip's War. Central Falls holds concerts here on Sunday during the summer, when you can also climb the tower and take in excellent views of the valley. At any time of day, you'll find walking trails ideal for a light stroll.

A short walk southwest of the park is the **Lysander and Susan Flagg Museum and Cultural Center** (209 Central St., 401/727-7440, www.cflibrary.org/flaggmuseum.htm, by appointment, free). This stately colonial revival home contains maps, newspapers, paintings, and photos relevant to the city's history as well as a collection of locally produced textiles. If you are interested in the collection, call ahead, as it is open only by appointment.

Cumberland and Lincoln

Cumberland offers a quieter and more rural vision of the Blackstone River Valley. Extensive mineral deposits, mostly iron and copper, provided early revenue for the town, but today Cumberland prospers with revenues from light manufacturing and retail. In Valley Falls, an old mill community in the southwest section of Cumberland, you can visit the **Valley Falls Heritage Park** (45 Broad St., Cumberland, 401/334-9996, free). This self-guided historic trail occupies the site of the former Valley Falls Company, which produced great amounts of textiles from the 1810s through the 1930s. There is no formal museum or guided tours, but a network of paths, ramps, and bridges traverses the property, and interpretative signs describe how different parts of the mill functioned.

From here, it's a five-mile drive north on Route 114 to reach family-owned **Diamond**

Hill Vineyards (3145 Diamond Hill Rd., Cumberland, 401/333-2751 or 800/752-505, www.favorlabel.com, tours and tastings noon–5 P.M. Thurs.–Sat., 11 A.M.–3 P.M. Sun.). Since 1976, the winery has been producing acclaimed pinot noir along with traditional New England wines made with blueberries, peaches, and apples. You can tour the grounds and winery, which are anchored by an 18th-century farmhouse. Also nearby, just 3.5 miles farther north, is Diamond Hill Park, on Route 114, which offers very nice views of the Rhode Island and southern Massachusetts countryside from its summit.

Named in 1871 for the 16th U.S. president, Lincoln was once the home of Narragansett Indians and later the settler William Blackstone, for whom the river is named. At Blackstone State Park in the Quinnville section of Lincoln, you can learn about the riverboats that plied the Blackstone Canal as well as other forms of transportation in the valley at the Captain Wilbur Kelly House Transportation Museum (Lower River Rd., 401/333-0295, 9 A.M.–4:30 P.M. daily Apr.–Oct.).

WOONSOCKET

Barely a blip on the radar screen during Rhode Island's first 200 years, Woonsocket (population 43,000) developed during the mid-19th century into one of the nation's great hubs of woolen manufacture. The industry thrived well into the 1940s before succumbing to increased costs and competition from cheaper labor in the South. Today the city celebrates its labor history and strong French-Canadian heritage with the Museum of Work and Culture, one of the most fascinating and well-executed museums in the Northeast. Apart from it and the city's abundance of nicely preserved mill buildings, there are relatively few formal attractions here, but Woonsocket does offer visitors a glimpse of an industrial community relatively little changed in the past century.

Woonsocket may take its name from the Native American word *nisowosaket,* which translates roughly as "thunder mist," but there's some debate as to the legitimacy of this derivation. As trade among southern New England's major metropolitan areas began to flourish in the early 1800s, Woonsocket's star began to rise, first as a major stopover on the stage road from Hartford to Boston. The fast-flowing Blackstone River and its numerous tributaries provided power for dozens of Woonsocket mills during the city's peak years of production. Sluiceways branched out from the rivers and ran alongside streets and rail tracks, over viaducts, and into the basements of factory buildings. After an especially acute industrial boom after the Civil War, Woonsocket found itself with more factories than it could fill with workers. It welcomed workers from Quebec in Canada and then from many other countries.

You can still hear a French-Canadian accent in these parts, although distinctive intonations and words fade a little with each generation. Walk around downtown and the residential neighborhoods surrounding it and you'll see African Americans, Asians, Portuguese, Latin Americans, French Canadians, and people of many other ethnicities. The city abounds with grand, often formidable stone-and-redbrick industrial architecture, the framework of a once-vibrant factory town. Along many streets you'll pass imposing stick, Queen Anne, and gingerbread Victorian houses, most of them subdivided, as well as hundreds of southern New England's trademark triple-decker houses.

Market Square

You can get a real sense of the city's industrial heritage around Market Square, which overlooks Woonsocket Falls and lies within steps of numerous old factory buildings. Because of horrendous floods through the years, mechanical flood barriers were installed in 1955 by the Army Corps of Engineers—these now diminish the view of the 30-foot falls as they appeared before their energy was first harnessed. But as they rush below the Main Street Bridge, they still make quite a racket and produce a cool mist. Across the bridge, you'll see the turbine building where the Blackstone Electric Company's Thunder Mist Plant produces

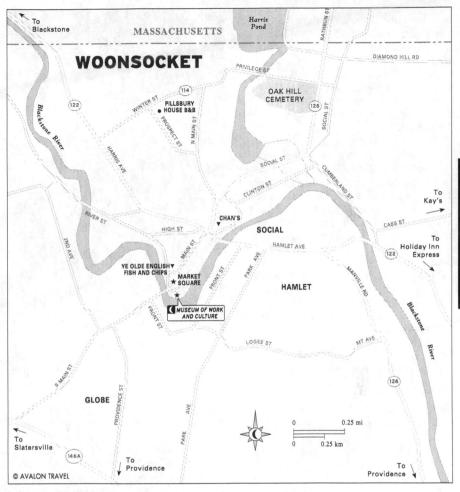

hydroelectric power. The falls produce more than 7 million kilowatt-hours of electricity per year. You can also see one of the old yarn mills just off Market Square. The names of many shops and on the sides of buildings display the city's French-Canadian ties.

◖ Museum of Work and Culture

The Rhode Island Historical Society's Museum of Work and Culture (42 S. Main St., 401/769-9675, www.rihs.org, 9:30 A.M.–4 P.M. Tues.–Fri., 10 A.M.–5 P.M. Sat., 1–4 P.M. Sun., $7)

anchors Market Square and provides a wonderfully vivid glimpse into the industrial history of Woonsocket and southern New England. The curators have beautifully designed imaginative, interactive exhibits that capture the spirit and reveal the hardships of the city's history.

Specifically, the museum traces the history of Woonsocket's French-Canadian immigration. You can get a very good sense of this insular community, its proud labor history, and its ardent preservation of customs and language. Among other things, exhibits recreate a 1920s textile mill shop, a farmhouse in rural Quebec, and a circa-1900 Catholic church. One of the better exhibits takes you into a triple-decker—these three-story tenements were mostly built from the 1890s to about 1930 and are notable for their stacked three-story exterior porches; they're a common sight throughout urban Rhode Island and in many other parts of New England.

The museum tour ends with a presentation inside a recreated 1930s Independent Textile Union Hall. The ITU was founded in Woonsocket in 1931 by Joseph Schmetz, a Belgian worker and socialist; it preceded the AFL-CIO and at its peak had a membership as large as 18,000, representing every craft and industry. Many of the tapes and interactive exhibits are narrated by older town residents who lived through the city's labor strife of the early 20th century. You can read some of the touching letters immigrants sent back to their families in rural Quebec. In one important respect, the Museum of Work and Culture succeeds where many of the famous mansions and historical societies elsewhere in the state fail: It actually talks with its visitors rather than merely showing them static displays or reeling off facts.

Bernon Street

Running east from Market Square, Bernon Street brings you alongside **River Island Park,** where a walking path traces one of the old trenches that carried water from the falls to factories decades ago. This is the heart of **Old Woonsocket Falls Village;** downriver a bit (a left from Bernon St. onto Front St.) is **Old Bernon Village,** home to several fine old cotton mills. Over the Court Street Bridge, you can take in a very nice view of the old Bernon Mills.

The Providence and Worcester rail bridge, supported by the original 1847 stone pillars, crosses the Woonsocket River downstream from the Court Street Bridge. At Depot Square is the 1882 **Worcester Railroad Depot** (1 Depot Sq., 401/762-0250, www.nps.gov/blac, 8 A.M.–7 P.M. Mon.–Fri., free) which replaced

an exhibit at the Museum of Work and Culture

the wooden original, lost in a fire. Trains no longer stop here (although two freight trains pass by nightly), but the impressive station functions as the headquarters of the Blackstone River Valley National Heritage Corridor Commission. Inside are exhibits and documents about the Blackstone River Valley; park rangers can answer questions about the area's history.

Some of industrial Rhode Island's most notable commercial buildings line Woonsocket's Main Street, including the imposing **City Hall** (169 Main St.), where Abraham Lincoln once spoke. It was built in 1856 and added on to in 1891. Several vintage early-20th-century buildings line the street nearby. Some of these have been restored, and others have not, but there is great potential for full restoration. Many of the city's mills now house light industry and service-oriented companies.

North Smithfield

Just west of Woonsocket, North Smithfield, a rural community during its earliest years, incorporated in 1871, when it had become an

THE FRENCH CANADIANS OF WOONSOCKET

By the 1870s, the bustling mill town of Woonsocket had virtually no unemployment and an almost desperate need for new workers. Many factory owners had become nervous about hiring more American workers, as they were starting to speak up angrily about the mills' brutal working conditions. The population in nearby rural Quebec, Canada, depended largely on farming, but the area had a short growing season, meaning they accepted the long hours and poor living conditions of the mill towns without much complaint. The intensely close-knit French Canadians mingled little with workers from other backgrounds, which weakened the solidarity of Woonsocket's factory employees. Many Irish, Scottish, and English immigrants also came to work Woonsocket's mills during these years, but if they complained too much about their jobs, they could easily be replaced by more French Canadians.

Most French Canadian workers in Woonsocket were from small Quebec towns, but large numbers also came from Quebec City and Trois-Rivières. One of the largest French-Canadian populations thrived in Woonsocket, despite the local Yankees and many other immigrants who continued to disparage them for accepting work for the lowest wages and filling most of the jobs.

Their insularity kept their community cohesive for many generations. The social hub of close-knit French Canadian Woonsocket was the appropriately named neighborhood of Social. By 1940 people of French Canadian descent made up 75 percent of the overall population of Woonsocket, and the majority of residents spoke with one another in French. Until 1942 the city produced La Tribune, a French-language newspaper, and radio station WOON (then WWON) broadcast in French into the mid-1960s. Still today on some local radio stations you can hear programs spoken in the Quebecois French dialect.

The city celebrates its heritage in other ways: A handful of restaurants serve authentic French Canadian fare such as poutine, French fries with hot chicken gravy and cheese, and ragout de pattes, fresh pork hocks browned with flour and served with vegetables.

OUTSIDE PROVIDENCE

industrial stronghold like the rest of the region. Its historic mill towns include **Union Village** (southwest of the Woonsocket border off Rte. 146A, just 1.5 miles north of the intersection of Rtes. 146A and 104), which contains a number of fine old homes and makes for a pretty drive—most of the oldest buildings date to the 1790s and early 1800s.

From Union Village, continue northwest along Route 146A for about two miles, and turn left onto Green Street to reach historic **Slatersville,** the first planned industrial community in the country. Along with nearby Forestdale, once a mostly Polish and Portuguese factory hub that produced everything from scythes to flannel blankets, it was among the most prolific mill villages of the day. Slatersville was a continuation of the region's "great experiment" in mill industrialization.

The Slater mill complex in Pawtucket required no construction of housing and village buildings because it sat in the middle of an already established urban enclave, but Slatersville was created in a then-rural area west of Woonsocket. John Slater, the younger brother of Samuel, had come to the United States in 1803; Samuel hired him to scout out a site along a strong source of water power that would be suitable for the creation of a full-fledged mill village. He chose to build around a small existing settlement, then known as Buffum's Mills, and in 1807 they opened a mill. They also built a village of worker housing, which today remains remarkably intact. This charming little mill village offers a glimpse of the blueprint for so many villages around New England.

From Slatersville, take Main Street west to Route 102, which leads southwest into Burrillville.

Burrillville

Established in 1730 and incorporated as a town in 1806, Burrillville today is geographically one of the largest towns in the state, occupying about 55 square miles and comprising several old mill communities. By the 1850s, Burrillville was the state's most prolific producer of wool goods. Production peaked around the turn of the 20th century and then declined steadily through the next few decades. Most of the mills had packed up and moved south by the 1960s, and today these little vestiges of industrial life look rather dated and even deserted. The town is also a center of recreational activity thanks to its several lakes and nature preserves. As in Woonsocket and North Smithfield, Burrillville is home to many people of French-Canadian origin.

Some of the abandoned mills are interesting just to look at. In **Harrisville**, for instance, you'll drive by the old Stillwater Worsted Mills, which at the time of its construction was the largest concrete building in the country. Now the site is slowly being renovated into a modern mixed-use complex by the town, which recently opened a new library here and is working to bring a condo complex beneath the old clock tower. Even in its half-desolate state, you can stand here imagining the bustle of this village when hundreds of workers lived and toiled here.

Burrillville's mills are famous for having clothed a huge chunk of the Union Army during the Civil War and dressing U.S. soldiers during both World Wars. Quite a few buildings in Providence were made with granite quarried from Burrillville. It's one of the better towns in Rhode Island for leaf-peeping in the fall.

Smithfield

Not to be confused with North Smithfield, Smithfield (population 20,000)—which was settled as a Quaker enclave—lies just to the south and is its own incorporated entity. It also has a few small mill villages, but it's more a middle-class bedroom community for Providence commuters as well as home to **Bryant College** (1150 Douglas Pike,

401/232-6000 or 800/622-7001, www.bryant. edu), known to football fans as the summer training camp for the New England Patriots. Although the town developed heavily during the industrial revolution as a textiles center, it has always had strong agrarian roots and a reputation for apple farming; quite a few apple orchards still exist today. More recently, big-name corporate concerns have built modern offices in Smithfield, the largest being Fidelity Investments.

ENTERTAINMENT AND EVENTS
Performing Arts

The **Sandra Feinstein-Gamm Theatre** (172 Exchange St., Pawtucket, 401/723-4266, www.gammtheatre.org) presents five plays per year, including works by up-and-coming playwrights as well as established icons such as Tom Stoppard, Anton Chekhov, and Shakespeare. Recently restored in Woonsocket is the magnificent 1926 **Stadium Theatre Performing Arts Centre** (28 Monument Sq., Main St., Woonsocket, 401/762-4545, www.stadiumtheatre.com), which seats 1,100 and hosts live music, ballet and dance, children's theater, and cabaret. The success of this space has been a great boon to the region.

The **Blackstone River Theatre** (549 Broad St., Cumberland, 401/725-9272, www.riverfolk.org) is a nonprofit cultural center that presents music, dance, and folk arts, usually in the traditions of the many different ethnic groups that have settled in the Blackstone River Valley. Many presentations are geared toward children. The theater occupies a vintage former Masonic Lodge that had been slated for demolition until the theater company took it over in 1996.

Although based in Pawtucket, the **All Children's Theatre** (255 Main St., Suite 201, Pawtucket, 401/728-1222, www.act-inri.org) produces works at several locales, including the Vartan Gregorian School (455 Wickenden St., Providence), the Boys and Girls Club of Pawtucket Arts Center (210 Main St., Pawtucket), and other locales in Barrington,

East Greenwich, and Kingston. This outstanding company formed in 1987 to produce fine theater for, by, and with young people.

Nightlife

In Woonsocket, it's hard to find a more unusual and entertaining venue than **Chan's** (267 Main St., Woonsocket, 401/765-1900, www.chanseggrollsandjazz.com, 11:30 A.M.–10 P.M. Mon.–Wed., 11:30 A.M.–10:30 P.M. Thurs. and Sat., 11:30 A.M.–12:30 A.M. Fri. and Sun., $5–14), which brings in a great variety of jazz bands and musicians, especially on weekdays. Head to East Providence to tickle your funny bone at the **Comedy Connection** (39 Warren Ave., East Providence, 401/438-8383, www.ricomedyconnection.com), which features a steady roster of humorists and comics.

Events

Culture vultures should check out the **Pawtucket Arts Festival** (401/724-5200, www.pawtucketartsfestival.org), which runs from the last weekend in August to the last weekend in September at various places around Pawtucket. The first weekend's festivities are mostly around Slater Mill, and the second weekend around Slater Park. Eat a French-Canadian meat pie as you browse wood carvings, photography exhibitions, and more.

In Woonsocket, **Autumnfest** takes hold in early October at World War II Memorial Park (Social St., Woonsocket, 401/762-6400), with four days of live music and entertainment, amusement rides, fireworks, a Columbus Day parade, and foods of all kinds.

Befitting a region rife with arts and crafts galleries, the **Scituate Art Festival** (www.scituateartfestival.org) attracts more than 100,000 enthusiasts every Columbus Day weekend to the 200 stalls set up along the Village Green and the several handsome streets that emanate from the main drag, Route 116. Come to enjoy the live music and great food.

Through most of December, you can attend the **Winter Wonderland at Slater Park** (Armistice Blvd., Pawtucket, 401/726-3185, www.pawtucketwinterwonderland.org), a

miniature winter village set up on the park grounds. It includes live entertainment, clowns, snacks, and hayrides at the Looff Carousel. In early May, a similar day of festivities kicks off the spring opening of the Looff Carousel. On Christmas Eve, Slatersville comes alive with holiday lights and luminarias for an evening stroll through this picturesque village.

In mid-May, head to Woonsocket's lively River Island Park, at Market Square, for the **Annual Riverfest and Friends of the Blackstone Canoe/Kayak Race** (401/334-5003, www.blackstoneriver.org). The 4.2-mile race runs from downtown Woonsocket to Mannville, and the park hosts food stalls, live music, and crafts.

SHOPPING

A longtime favorite destination in Cumberland, **Phantom Farms** (2920 Diamond Hill Rd., 401/333-2240, 6:30 A.M.–6:30 P.M. Mon.–Fri., 7 A.M.–6 P.M. Sat.–Sun.) has a greenhouse gift shop and offers pick-your-own veggies, pumpkins, apples, and other fruits seasonally, along with fresh-baked pies, apple crisp, candied apples, and other gourmet goodies. During the holidays, it's also a great source of Christmas trees, wreaths, and other decorations, and there are Easter egg hunts and other family-oriented events in the spring. There's also a playground for kids.

In North Smithfield, **Wright's Dairy Farm and Bakery** (200 Woonsocket Hill Rd., 401/767-3014 or 877/227-9734, www.wrightsdairyfarm.com, 8 A.M.–7 P.M. Mon.–Sat., 8 A.M.–4 P.M. Sun.) is a working farm where you can view cow-milking daily and buy fresh milk, whipping cream, cream-filled pastries, and baked goods from the on-site shop. In the early 1970s they started a bakery, which has supplemented the farm's income and sells a vast range of cakes, cookies, and sweets (try the coconut cream pie or shortbread cookies).

It's only appropriate that Pawtucket would have one of the better fabric shops in the state. **Lorraine Mills Fabrics** (593 Mineral Springs Ave., 401/722-9500, 10 A.M.–6 P.M. Mon.–Sat., noon–5 P.M. Sun.) offers thousands of bolts of fabric and is set inside a historic brick mill building. Knitters and darners will also want to check out the **Yarn Outlet** (225 Conant St., Pawtucket, 401/722-5600, www.theyarnoutlet.com, 9 A.M.–4:30 P.M. Mon.–Fri.), which has needles, books, yarns, and fabrics.

In the Greenville section of Smithfield, the **Greenville Antique Center** (711 Putnam Pike, U.S. 44, 401/949-4999, 10 A.M.–5 P.M. Fri.–Mon. and Wed., 10 A.M.–7 P.M. Thurs.) displays the wares of about 140 dealers, offering everything from furniture, toys, china, and glassware to vintage prints and paintings.

A 10–15-minute drive northeast of Woonsocket or Providence, **Wrentham Village Premium Outlets** (U.S. 1 at I-495, Wrentham, MA, 508/384-0600, www.premiumoutlets.com/Wrentham, 10 A.M.–9 P.M. Mon.–Sat., 10 A.M.–6 P.M. Sun.) includes about 170 branches of major-name stores, among them Banana Republic, Barneys New York, Bebe, Brooks Brothers, Burberry, Calvin Klein, Coach, DKNY Jeans, Ferragamo, Gap, Guess, Hugo Boss, J. Crew, J. Jill, Kenneth Cole, Nautica, Nike, Perry Ellis, Ralph Lauren, Sony, Timberland, and Williams-Sonoma.

SPORTS AND RECREATION
◖ PawSox

New Englanders root for the Boston Red Sox, but Rhode Islanders get behind their scrappy PawSox (McCoy Stadium, 1 Columbus Ave., Pawtucket, 401/724-7300, www.pawsox.com) with particular fervor. For a fraction of what they're charging up in Beantown, you can score great seats for a game of this Triple-A farm team that has been home to the rising stars Jason Varitek, Roger Clemens, Wade Boggs, Nomar Garciaparra, and countless others. The regular season runs April–early September, and you can also hear the games on the radio at 790 AM.

◖ Kayaking the Blackstone

The same powerful current that ran the mills also makes the Blackstone River a great spot for kayaking and, especially in spring when the river rises, white-water rafting. The Blackstone is a complex waterway for paddlers; you'll encounter dams, which require portaging, and unmarked spillways that can greatly alter the river's water level. Rangers at the **Blackstone River Valley National Heritage Corridor** (1 Depot Sq., 401/762-0250, www.nps.gov/blac, 8 A.M.–4:30 P.M. Mon.–Fri.) offer a great deal of information on how to make the most of canoeing and kayaking as well as how to do so safely. You can also learn a great deal about the river's history, and the flora and fauna encountered along it.

Before boating on the river, visit the website of the United States Geological Survey monitoring station (http://waterdata.usgs.gov), which is in Northbridge, Massachusetts. From here you can get a good indication of whether the flow is safe.

To familiarize the public with the Blackstone River, the National Heritage Corridor and the Rhode Island Canoe and Kayak Association have created the **Blackstone Valley Paddle Club** (401/762-0440, www.ricka.org), which offers rentals on the first and third Tuesday of every month. The club offers kayak and canoe lessons and organized excursions led by park rangers, and also advice and information on taking to the river in these parts. You can also participate in water-quality monitoring projects, river and canal clean-ups, and other activities that promote the health of this valuable resource. Guided paddles are typically given through the summer at 6:30 P.M. on Tuesday and Wednesday. Putting-in points along the river change each week, so call ahead for details. On Saturdays, you can come by for lessons or to improve your kayaking and canoeing skills.

Bicycling, Jogging, and Inline Skating

The **Blackstone River Bikeway** follows parts of the Blackstone River and the old Blackstone Canal—it runs from Pawtucket 17 miles north to Woonsocket but will someday connect all the way to Worcester. Another connection is currently in the works to hook up with the East Bay path in order to create a continuous route of more than 30 miles of biking within the state. You can access it at several points, and you can park your car at lots in Lincoln (at both ends of Front Street, along the river) and at Blackstone State Park at the end of Lower River Road. It's a hit among bikers, inline skaters, joggers, and strollers. You'll pass by some of the great old mills of the region, as well as vast meadows and some fairly mundane suburban stretches.

You can also rent bikes in East Providence at **East Providence Cycle** (414 Warren Ave., 401/434-3838, www.eastprovidencecycle.com, 9 A.M.–6 P.M. Mon., 9 A.M.–8 P.M. Tues.–Fri., 9 A.M.–5:30 P.M. Sat., 11 A.M.–5 P.M. Sun.). Rental rates in the area run $25–50 for a full day.

Northwest of Providence in Lincoln, a favorite spot in the area for strolling, jogging, swimming, and having fun is **Lincoln Woods State Park** (2 Manchester Print Works Lane, off Rte. 123, 401/723-7892, www.riparks.com), also known as Lincoln Woods Reservation. Established in 1909 on Abraham Lincoln's birthday, the heavily wooded, gently rolling 627-acre park surrounds Olney Pond, which is popular for swimming, trout-fishing, and— when weather permits—ice-skating. Other features include playing fields, a snack bar, picnic tables and shelters, fireplaces, a bathhouse with changing rooms and showers, and a boat ramp.

ACCOMMODATIONS
$50-100

Just off I-95, the **Comfort Inn Providence/ Pawtucket** (2 George St., Pawtucket, 401/723-6700 or 877/424-6423, www.comfortinn.com, $99–175) has standard rooms in a typical midrise building; amenities include an outdoor pool, guest laundry, and continental breakfast. Attached is the Ground Round Restaurant.

A gorgeous Second Empire Victorian with a green mansard roof, the **Pillsbury House B&B** (341 Prospect St., Woonsocket, 401/766-7983 or 800/205-4112, www.pillsburyhouse.com, $95–135) is one of the most appealing inns in

northern Rhode Island and one of the better values in the state. The 1870s house with a big leafy yard sits along one of Woonsocket's most prestigious streets, lined with large homes that were once the domain of mill owners. It's an easy walk from downtown. Rooms are spacious and bright with mostly Victorian antiques that include ornate chandeliers, plush beds made up with either country quilts or fine white linens, and myriad antiques, and most of the rooms have soaring 10-foot ceilings and period wallpapers.

$100-150

Woonsocket is home to the well-maintained **Holiday Inn Express** (194 Fortin Dr., 401/769-5000 or 800/315-2621, www.hiexpress.com, $117–149), which has a convenient downtown location. This clean and efficiently run 88-room property has an indoor pool, a whirlpool, and a health club; there are also 16 suites.

In Smithfield, the **Quality Inn** (355 Rte. 116, Smithfield, 401/232-2400, www.qualityinn.com, $109–189) is another inexpensive, low-frills property. It has 117 rooms and an outdoor heated pool; rates include continental breakfast.

One of the better chain properties in the region, the 84-unit **Holiday Inn Express** (1010 Douglas Pike, Rte. 7, Smithfield, 401/231-6300 or 800/315-2621, www.hiexpress.com, $100–139) has business services, a gym, and rooms with microwaves and refrigerators. Every morning there's complimentary coffee in the lobby.

$150-250

Certainly one of the most distinctive accommodations in New England, the English-built **Samuel Slater Canal Boat B&B** (Central Falls, 401/724-2200 or 800/454-2882, www.bedandbreakfastblackstone.com) was brought to Central Falls in 2000; the 40-foot boat offers a look back into the era when canals drove the economy in this region, about 1828–1848. The boat can be chartered by up to 12 passengers for tours along the river, or up to four can use the boat as an overnight B&B. Amenities include a TV and DVD player, a phone, and a full galley with a microwave; breakfast is delivered to your door in the morning.

FOOD

The region is dominated by fairly simple and affordable restaurants that emphasize steak, pastas, and the region's famous "family chicken dinners." With such a diversity of ethnicities in the region, you'll also find several fine purveyors of authentic Portuguese, Italian, and French-Canadian food.

Upscale

It's one of the few restaurants in northern Rhode Island that could be called dressy, but even at **Bella** (1992 Victory Sq., Burrillville, 401/568-6996, www.bellarestaurantandbanquet.com, 4–9 P.M. Tues.–Thurs., 11:30 A.M.–9 P.M. Fri., 4–10 P.M. Sat., noon–8 P.M. Sun., $9–24) you can get by with casual attire. The spacious dining room of this Italian restaurant looks and feels like a banquet hall—the ambience is not especially distinctive, but it's pleasant nonetheless. The menu has great variety, and specialties include grilled New York sirloin steak brushed with rosemary-infused oil and grilled marinated chicken over a tossed field greens with balsamic vinegar. Pastas, of course, are a great option: Homemade lasagna and gnocchi are favorites, and you can mix and match several types of pasta with about 15 kinds of sauce (red or white clam, vodka, primavera, and so on).

Pizza and Pub Grub

Justly famous for introducing northern Rhode Islanders to the communal concept of "family chicken dinners," **Wright's Farm Restaurant** (84 Inman Rd., Nasonville, 401/769-2856, www.wrightsfarm.com, 4–9 P.M. Thurs.–Fri., noon–9:30 P.M. Sat., noon–8 P.M. Sun., $8–14) presents family-style meals—the heaping platters of chicken, green salad, fries, rolls, and pasta sides can feed armies. The concept is so simple, so all-American: all-you-can-possibly-stuff-down-your-throat dinners that bring legions of family members and friends together in a homey ambience. It's a huge place, with banquet seating for 1,600 patrons, plus a gift and toy shop that sells house-made specialties such as Italian dressing, barbecue sauce, fudge, and pasta sauce. It has become increasingly famous every year since it opened in 1972. It's

KENYON'S GRIST MILL

Rhode Islanders love their jonnycakes, and probably the most famous purveyor of the main ingredient of jonnycake batter, stone-ground cornmeal, is **Kenyon's Grist Mill** (21 Glen Rock Rd., just off Rte. 138, five miles east of I-95 exit 3, West Kingston, 401/783-4054 or 800/753-6966, www.kenyonsgristmill.com). The Kenyon Corn Meal Company has been milling grist since the early 1700s, and the current operations are in a charmingly raffish clapboard building with peeling red paint that dates to 1886. It looks about like it must have more than a century ago, and the staff still grinds the meal the traditional way, using a massive granite millstone—it's great fun for visitors to watch the staff make the meal using a process that's remarkably similar to that which the indigenous people of New England did for centuries before Europeans arrived.

The mill employs ancient techniques but often comes up with new meals and grains, which it grinds without any preservatives or additives. So whether you're an amateur baker or a real pro, or you just want to try making jonnycakes at home, this is the definitive source for meals and flours. Some favorite Kenyon's Grist Mill products, in addition to jonnycake meal, include buckwheat flour, scotch oat flour, buttermilk-honey pancake mix, quince jam, cinnamon apple jelly, whole quinoa, Rhode Island flint corn, Indian pudding, and local honey.

a pretty amazing operation—75 ovens work away in the kitchen.

Another excellent chicken-dinner purveyor in northern Rhode Island is **Village Haven** (90 School St., Forestdale, 401/762-4242, www.thevillagehaven.com, 4–8:30 P.M. Wed.–Thurs., 4–9 P.M. Fri.–Sat., noon–8 P.M. Sun., $8–14), which scores high marks for its down-home American cooking such as prime beef and baked stuffed jumbo shrimp. The cinnamon buns are the stuff of legend. It's a very lively spot, with friendly staff and dependable food.

At **Ye Olde English Fish and Chips** (Market Sq., Woonsocket, 401/762-3637, 10 A.M.–8 P.M. daily, $2–7), you can grab your food and eat it on a bench overlooking the Blackstone River and falls, or eat in the casual sit-down dining room. This place has been serving fresh seafood since 1922, and its proximity to the Rhode Island Museum of Work and Culture makes it a hit with visitors. Of course, fish-and-chips are the menu favorite, but you might also try a fish burger, stuffed quahogs, baked scallops, baked stuffed shrimp, or Manhattan-style clam chowder.

Set in a grove of towering pine trees in North Smithfield, the aptly named **Pines Restaurant** (1204 Pound Hill Rd., 401/766-2122, www.thepinesrestaurant.com, 4:30–8:30 P.M. Thurs., 4–9 P.M. Fri.–Sat., noon–8 P.M. Sun., $7–16) is another favorite for family-style chicken as well as traditional American standbys such as lobster, prime rib, baked haddock, king crab legs, and chops. It's family-un and tends to draw a local crowd.

Slatersville's best dining option is **Pinelli's Cucina** (900 Victory Hwy., 401/767-2444, www.pinellimarrarestaurants.com, 11:30 A.M.–10 P.M. daily, $14–21), where you might sample both classic and contemporary Italian fare, such as scampi over capellini, veal topped with prosciutto and mozzarella with a mushroom marsala sauce, and grilled Italian pork chops with sautéed vinegar peppers and Tuscan potato wedges.

In Cumberland, **Tuck's** (2352 Mendon Rd., 401/658-0450, 11 A.M.–11 P.M. Mon.–Sat.,

3–8 P.M. Sun., $6–13) is a reliable option for burgers, salads, chicken wraps, homemade soups, fish-and-chips, and other tavern fare. The bar also serves 12 kinds of beers on tap, making it a favorite watering hole for locals. There's a popular outdoor deck too.

Ethnic Fare

Somewhat Americanized but plenty of fun is **Chan's** (267 Main St., Woonsocket, 401/765-1900, www.chanseggrollsandjazz.com, 11:30 A.M.–10 P.M. Mon.–Wed., 11:30 A.M.–10:30 P.M. Thurs. and Sat., 11:30 A.M.–12:30 A.M. Fri. and Sun., $5–14), an elaborate, almost campy Chinese restaurant that since 1905 has been noted perhaps more for its live entertainment than anything else. It's well regarded enough that people will drive 30 minutes or more to check out the scene here, sample the tasty Szechuan fare, and listen to the line-up of hip jazz greats and other musicians. The menu is encyclopedic, with nods to just about every Chinese culinary tradition you can think of. Specialties include roast pork egg foo yong, beef sautéed with pickled ginger, egg drop soup, lobster with fried rice, and the inevitable Tahitian Delight (fresh sea scallops and tender chicken stir-fried in a light sauce with straw mushrooms, broccoli, carrot slices, and water chestnuts on a bed of pan-fried noodles).

At the Lincoln Mall, **Asia Grille** (off Route 146 and I-295, 401/334-3200, www.asiagrille.com, 11 A.M.–9:30 P.M. Sun.–Thurs., 11 A.M.–10:30 A.M. Fri.–Sun., $5–15) serves a well-prepared if fairly standard range of Chinese and other pan-Asian specialties, such as hot-and-sour soup, shrimp with almonds, and General Tso's chicken. It's an attractive spot with hanging Chinese prints, tapestries, and regional artwork.

East Providence has one of the state's several outstanding Portuguese restaurants, **Madeira** (288 Warren Ave., 401/431-1322, www.madeirarestaurant.com, 11:30 A.M.–10 P.M. Mon.–Thurs., 11:30 A.M.–11 P.M. Fri.–Sat., noon–10 P.M. Sun., $10–21), a classy spot with a highly solicitous staff. Here you can try flame-grilled Portuguese sausage; kale, chorizo, and potato soup; fillet of scrod topped with the restaurant's secret Madeira sauce; paella Valencia; and boiled dried codfish served with boiled potatoes, chickpeas, and hard-boiled egg. Everything is cooked to order, which means you'll often have to wait 30–40 minutes for your dinner, but it's worth the wait for such authentic fare. Vegetarian entrées are available on request.

Quick Bites

In Woonsocket, drop by **Kay's** (1013 Cass Ave., 401/762-9675, $3–10) for superb sandwiches and like fare—the huge steak sandwich is a specialty, and there is a fine lobster roll. The kitchen serves till midnight.

Modern Diner (364 East Ave., Pawtucket, 401/726-8390, 6 A.M.–3 P.M. Mon.–Sat., under $7), a crimson-and-cream Sterling Streamliner steel railroad-car diner attached to a Victorian house, serves excellent home-style food. It's a short drive from Slater Mill, and breakfast is served all day. Plenty of the state's diner aficionados rank this place among the best around. Cranberry-almond pancakes are a highlight, but you'll find a full slate of typical diner favorites. It's not open for dinner and accepts cash only.

For several decades, devotees of burgers and fries have been cramming into **Stanley's** (535 Dexter Ave., Central Falls, 401/726-9689, www.stanleyshamburgers.com, 11 A.M.–8 P.M. Mon.–Thurs., 11 A.M.–9 P.M. Fri.–Sat., $3–7); the patties here are freshly made and wonderful, grilled with several toppings (cheddar, mushrooms, onions); the French fries are prepared with just the right crispness.

Horton's Seafood (809 Broadway, East Providence, 401/434-3116, 11 A.M.–8 P.M. Wed.–Thurs., 10 A.M.–9 P.M. Fri., 11 A.M.–8 P.M. Sat., $4–11) serves tasty lobster rolls that can be admired for both their heft and lack of filler. In summer you can dine on the screened-in porch.

Get ice cream kicks at **Sunshine Creamery** (305 N. Broadway, East Providence, 401/431-2828, noon–10 P.M. Sun.–Thurs., noon–11 P.M.

Fri.–Sat., $2–5), which dishes out nearly 40 flavors of the sweet, frozen treat.

Ice Cream Machine (4288 Diamond Hill Rd., Cumberland, 401/333-5053, www.icecreampie.com, 11 A.M.–10 P.M. daily Apr.–oct., under $4) is one of the top homemade ice cream shops in the state, also known for its ice-cream pies.

Technically in Pawtucket but literally a few steps from the Providence border is a prosaic shopping center that has several delicious options for cheap eats. The top picks are **Rasoi** (727 East Ave., Pawtucket, 401/728-5500, www.rasoi-restaurant.com, 11:30 A.M.–10:30 P.M. Mon.–Sat., 11:30 A.M.–9:30 P.M. Sun., $6–14), a brightly colored, good-quality Indian eatery with fast service and an eclectic, tasty menu. The kitchen focuses on coastal Indian regions, where boiling and steaming are preferred to frying, so dishes are flavorful but also healthful. Next door is an attractive little veggie eatery called **Garden Grille** (727 East Ave., Pawtucket, 401/726-2826, www.gardengrillecafe.com, 10 A.M.–9:30 P.M. Mon.–Sat., 11 A.M.–8 P.M. Sun., $3–8), with a full juice bar, healthful goat cheese and arugula salads, fresh sandwiches, and all manner of great food. Also check out **Ronzio Pizza and Subs** (727 East Ave., 401/722-5530, 11 A.M.–10 P.M. Sun.–Thurs., 11 A.M.–11 P.M. Fri.–Sat., $9–17)—a locally owned chain of pretty good pizzerias, known for its Florentine chicken pizza (with plenty of spinach), steak arrabiata pizza, and two-foot calzones.

INFORMATION AND SERVICES
Visitor Information

Pamphlets, brochures, and visitor information are available on the towns north and northwest of Providence from the **Blackstone Valley Tourism Council** (175 Main St., Pawtucket, 401/724-2200 or 800/454-2882, www.tourblackstone.com).

Tours

One interesting way to explore the region is on

one of the cruises offered on the **Blackstone Valley Explorer** (175 Main St., Pawtucket, 401/724-2200, www.rivertourblackstone.com, $10 adults, $8 children), a 49-passenger riverboat with a canopy roof that runs up and down the Blackstone River June–mid-October. Several kinds of excursions are offered, departing from Central Falls and Woonsocket. Some of these are available only to groups and students, so it's best to call ahead for details. These tours give a particularly strong sense of the mix of rural and wildlife-inhabited lands that exist side-by-side with the great old mill villages of the past two centuries.

Another possibility is the **Conway Gray Line** (10 Nate Whipple Hwy., Cumberland, 401/658-3400 or 800/888-4661, www.conwaytours.com), which offers narrated van tours of the valley that pass by attractions both in Providence and Slater Mill as well as the many industrial sites of the area. The same company also operates a 33-passenger vintage-style trolley that can be chartered for tours; call for schedule information.

The most intriguing tour option is a tour on the *Samuel Slater* **Canal Boat** (401/724-2200 or 800/454-2882, www.tourblackstone.com/canal.htm), a bright red-and-green vintage canal boat. Built in Cambridgeshire, England, it can be chartered for tours along the Blackstone River and can also be booked as a bed-and-breakfast. It has seating for 12 and overnight accommodations for up to four guests. Charter rates are quite reasonable if you have a large group—it's $190 for the first 90 minutes and $75 each additional hour. Also offered are onboard clambakes, which cost $85 for two, $155 for four.

GETTING THERE AND AROUND

As for the surrounding area, the Blackstone River Valley is easy to get around by car, although you can take the bus to several places, among them Pawtucket and Woonsocket. It's fairly easy to get to Slater Mill from Providence using public transportation—Bus 99 is your best bet; it runs regularly between Kennedy Plaza in Providence and downtown Pawtucket. If you're driving, note that I-295 cuts across the southeastern half of the Blackstone River Valley as it loops from I-95 south of Providence back up to I-95 north of it in Attleboro, Massachusetts. From Providence, Route 146 is a quick limited-access highway northwest to Woonsocket.

Warwick and Cranston

On the opposite side of Providence from the Blackstone River Valley, Rhode Island's most densely populated suburbs, Warwick and Cranston, lie immediately south of the capital and contain high concentrations of indoor and strip malls, chain restaurants and motels, and busy roads lined with traffic lights. Warwick is also home to T. F. Green Airport, New England's third-busiest. Although it's crowded and in many places prosaic, this patch of middle-class upper-middle-class bedroom communities is not without charm. Both towns lie along Narragansett Bay and have several interesting and historic residential neighborhoods

near the water. In Warwick especially, you'll find several villages with their own personalities, histories, and walkable commercial districts. The towns also contain the nearest public beaches to Providence, and just south of Warwick, the all-American community of East Greenwich has a delightfully charming downtown with hip eateries and a smattering of cool boutiques.

WARWICK

It's almost incorrect to call Warwick a suburb—this full-fledged city is one of the state's most prominent communities, as it's home to Rhode Island's main airport and has

OUTSIDE PROVIDENCE

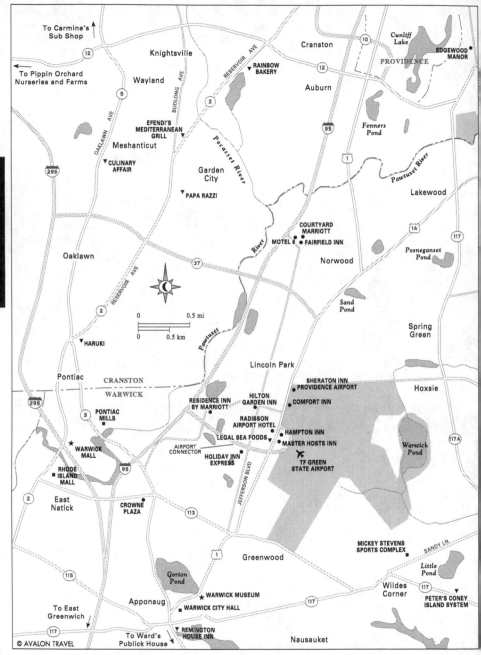

© AVALON TRAVEL

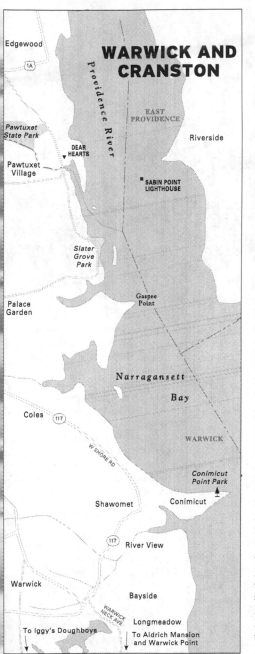

WARWICK AND CRANSTON

Edgewood

1A

Providence River

EAST
PROVIDENCE

Pawtuxet
State Park

Riverside

DEAR
HEARTS

Pawtuxet
Village

SABIN POINT
LIGHTHOUSE

Slater
Grove
Park

Gaspee
Point

Palace
Garden

Narragansett

Bay

Coles
117

WARWICK

W SHORE RD

Conimicut
Point Park

Shawomet

Conimicut

117

River View

Warwick

Bayside

WARWICK
NECK AVE

Longmeadow

To Iggy's Doughboys

To Aldrich Mansion
and Warwick Point

a population of about 85,000 (second only to Providence). Like many of the state's communities, Warwick actually comprises a slew of small village centers rather than one coherent core. Through the early 20th century, textile mills engaged in dyeing, bleaching, and finishing employed many of Warwick's workers, but even a century ago many residents commuted to Providence and other nearby towns, and it has remained a bedroom community ever since.

Apponaug Village

The city's civic center is historic Apponaug Village, where you'll find the dramatic 1894 **Warwick City Hall** (3275 Post Rd., U.S. 1, 401/738-2000, www.warwickri.gov), crowned with an imposing six-story clock tower. Practically next door, the **Warwick Museum of Art** (3259 Post Rd., U.S. 1, 401/737-0010, www.warwickmuseum.org, noon–4 P.M. Tues.–Sat., free), which was built in 1912 as the Kentish Artillery Armory, presents exceptionally interesting and well-curated rotating art and some history exhibits throughout the year. There are more than 30 buildings of historic or architectural distinction in the village; you can learn more about them by obtaining the free *Walking Tour of Historic Apponaug Village* booklet distributed by the Warwick Convention and Visitors Bureau, which produces a similar booklet on Pawtuxet Village.

Pawtuxet Village

Pawtuxet is Warwick's oldest village and contains a number of fine old colonial homes, most of them along Narragansett Avenue and the roads that intersect it. From Pawtuxet (not to be confused with Pawtucket, another city north of Providence) a party of local patriots attacked the grounded British revenue schooner *Gaspée,* one of several early acts of defiance against the crown in New England that ultimately led to the American Revolution. Since 1966 Pawtuxet has hosted the annual *Gaspée* Days celebration (401/781-1772, www.gaspee.org), held in late June,

OUTSIDE PROVIDENCE

COURTESY OF PROVIDENCE WARWICK CVB

Pawtuxet is Warwick's oldest village.

which features, among other events, a parade, a road race, fireworks, and a symbolic burning of the *Gaspée* in effigy.

Conimicut Village

An early fishing enclave that developed into a fashionable summer colony around the late 19th century, Conimicut Village has gradually become a laid-back, upper-middle-class suburb of attractive homes, many dating to the early part of the 20th century. There's great strolling along the bay and by Conimicut Park and Lighthouse, which pokes out into the Narragansett Bay and overlooks Patience and Prudence Islands. During Labor Day weekend, 30,000 people attend the Conimicut Festival, a lively crafts and food event. Just offshore from the village, **Conimicut Lighthouse** sits along a rocky ledge by Conimicut Point Park. You can't visit this 1868 structure, but it cuts a dashing figure in the bay. In 1960 the lighthouse was changed from kerosene to electric power—it was the last lighthouse in the nation to convert to electricity. In 2004 the city of Warwick acquired the lighthouse and

is currently working on restoring the interior with a grant from the national Department of Transportation, with the goal of eventually opening the building for tours.

Warwick has another impressive lighthouse at the tip of Warwick Neck. This 51-foot cast-iron tower was built in 1932 and was the last traditional lighthouse constructed in Rhode Island. It's now operated by the Coast Guard. Warwick Neck is one of the city's fanciest neighborhoods, the appropriate setting for one of the state's most imposing estates, even compared with those in Newport, the **Aldrich Mansion** (836 Warwick Neck Ave., 401/739-6850, www.aldrichmansion.com). This 75-acre estate on Narragansett Bay was the home of one of Rhode Island's greatest political figures, Senator Nelson W. Aldrich. On this estate, John D. Rockefeller Jr. married Aldrich's daughter, Abby, setting up one of the nation's more formidable political-industrial dynasties. The couple's son, Nelson Rockefeller, later served as vice president of the United States. It took more than 200 craftspeople more than 15 years to build this lavish 70-room mansion, which was completed in 1912. Today the mansion is rented out for weddings, business meetings, and other functions—it contains a fine collection of art, and all the original detailed woodwork has been carefully restored. The house starred alongside Brad Pitt in the 1998 film *Meet Joe Black.*

Potowomut

To reach one of the most interesting parts of Warwick, you have to get out of town. Potowomut occupies a peninsula south of Warwick proper on the shoreline of East Greenwich. You reach it by driving south of U.S. 1 through downtown East Greenwich, then make a left onto Forge Road, and another left onto Ives Road. Most of this land was used for raising cattle during colonial times, and Revolutionary War hero Nathanael Greene was born on the peninsula. At the tip of the peninsula is a small residential neighborhood with a mix of new and old homes, many of them overlooking the bay.

The big draw here is **Goddard Memorial State Park** (Ives Rd., 401/884-2010, free), the site of an ambitious tree-growing project undertaken by the late-19th-century owner of this land, Henry Russell, and continued by the subsequent owner, Colonel William Goddard. Today you can stroll or ride horseback through the park on many trails, admiring the fruits of their labors. There's also a fine beach along Greenwich Bay, numerous playing fields, bridle trails, picnic areas, changing facilities, and a nine-hole golf course. Concerts are given during the warmer months in the park's restored carousel pavilion, next to the beach.

CRANSTON

Cranston lies immediately southwest of Providence and is easily reached via I-95 or Route 10. The area was settled in 1638 by associates of Roger Williams, including William Harris, Zachariah Rhodes, and William Arnold (the progenitor of the traitorous Revolutionary War general Benedict Arnold). Harris waged a battle with Williams, asserting that his township was not under the jurisdiction of Providence. The land was then known as Pawtuxet, and in 1754 this and the adjacent settlements joined to form the town of Cranston (named for Samuel Cranston, governor of Rhode Island 1698–1727). It thrived as a textile-manufacturing center during the 19th and early 20th centuries.

ENTERTAINMENT AND EVENTS
Nightlife

Folks in Warwick and Cranston tend to have cocktails at restaurants with good bars attached, including **20 Water Street** (20 Water St., East Greenwich, 401/885-3703, www.twentywaterstreet.com), **Remington House Inn** (3376 Post Rd., Apponaug Village, 401/736-8388, www.theremingtonhouseinn.com), **Ward's Publick House** (3854 Post Rd., Warwick, 401/884-7008, www.wardspublickhouse.com), and **Legal Sea Foods** (2099 Post Rd., Warwick, 401/SEA-FOOD—401/732-3663, www.legalseafoods.com). The local outlet of bar-restaurants chain **Chelo's Waterfront Bar and Grille** (2225 Post Rd., Warwick, 401/737-7299, www.chelos.com) overlooks the bay. Head to **Copperfield's** (1551 Warwick Ave., Warwick, 401/738-7936) to shoot pool, watch a game on TV, belt out karaoke tunes, play darts, or listen to live bands—it's a large and popular hangout, sort of an adult's Chuck E. Cheese, with 10 pool tables and about a dozen large-screen TVs. There's often live folk, R&B, and rock at the **Harp and Shamrock** (557 Warwick Ave., 401/467-8998), a friendly, traditional Irish pub.

Events

Warwick's most celebrated event, *Gaspée Days* (401/781-1772), takes place toward the end of May and lasts well into June in Pawtuxet Village, in celebration of one of the American Revolution's earliest acts of defiance. Events include a huge arts and crafts fair, a gala ball in period colonial costume, a children's costume contest, a parade, and a mock battle reenactment.

In August, Rhode Island celebrates the region's French and French-Canadian heritage with **Pawtuxet Valley Franco-American Heritage Festival** (Majestic Park and Gazebo, Main St., West Warwick, 401/822-1232, www.franco-americanheritagefestival.org), with storytelling, regional cuisines, living-history exhibits, and live music.

SHOPPING

Warwick is a shopping hub for the state, although you won't necessarily find a huge number of independent stores. Still, if you're looking for the nearest outpost of your favorite chain, drive along Route 2, where you'll find Best Buy, Home Depot, Sam's Club, Sports Authority, T. J. Maxx, Barnes and Noble, Pier 1 Imports, Toys R Us, K-Mart, Newbury Comics, Staples, Petco, Bed Bath and Beyond, and a Christmas Tree Shop, among more than 200 others. Also along Route 2 are two large if fairly run-of-the-mill indoor shopping malls: the mid- to upscale **Warwick Mall** (400 Bald Hill Rd., Warwick, 401/739-7500, www.warwickmall.com, 10 A.M.–9 P.M. Mon.–Sat., 11 A.M.–6 P.M. Sun.), which is home to the

nation's largest Old Navy as well as branches of JCPenney, Macy's, Ann Taylor, Lane Bryant, Nine West, Zales, and the Disney Store; and the even more bland **Rhode Island Mall** (Rtes. 2 and 113, Warwick, 401/828-7651, 9:30 A.M.–9:30 P.M. Mon.–Sat., noon–6 P.M. Sun.), whose anchors include Sears, Kohl's, and Wal-Mart.

In Cranston, **Garden City Center** (Rte. 2, Cranston, 401/942-2800, www.gardencitycenter.com, 10 A.M.–9 P.M. Mon.–Sat., noon–6 P.M. Sun.) is an open-air shopping center with more than 70 upscale shops, including both local and chain operations. Good picks here include Banana Republic, Chico's, Crabtree and Evelyn, Eddie Bauer, Eastern Mountain Sports, J. Jill, Talbots, Victoria's Secret, and Williams-Sonoma.

Fans of antiques shopping should check out Warwick's **Antique Haven** (30 Post Rd., Warwick, 401/785-0327, 11:30 A.M.–5 P.M. daily) in historic Pawtuxet Village. Since 1910, the famed shop **Axelrod** (663 Killingly St., Johnston, 401/421-4833 or 888/429-3576) has been crafting fine musical instruments.

ANTIQUING

The towns in western Rhode Island tend to be fairly rural, with few formal attractions and shopping districts, but two charming exceptions have developed through the years: North Scituate and Chepachet. Both of these small historic villages contain a number of well-preserved 18th and 19th-century buildings, and both have become quite well known for their first-rate antiques shopping.

In the center of North Scituate village you'll find a nice range of antiques shops, including **J&M Hobbies** (180 Danielson Pike, North Scituate, 401/647-7778), a delightful nostalgic shop with vintage model railroad equipment, die-cast toy cars, crafts, puzzles, rockets, and other paraphernalia that may take you back to your childhood. **Village Antiques** (143 Danielson Pike, at Rte. 116, North Scituate, 401/647-7780) specializes in furnishings and decorative and fine arts from the mid-19th-

mid-20th centuries, from Victorian to arts and crafts to art deco.

In Chepachet, you can take classes at **Holidaze Stained Glass** (6B Money Hill Rd., Chepachet, 401/568-5140, www.holidazestainedglass.com), a studio where art and gifts in stained glass are sold and custom-made. **Magnolias and Memories** (171 Danielson Pike, Chepachet, 401/647-3335) occupies a fading Greek revival house and is piled high with collectibles, crafts, and country gifts. Almost everybody who visits Chepachet makes it a point to stop by the **Brown and Hopkins General Store** (1179 Putnam Pike, U.S. 44, Chepachet, 401/568-4830), which opened in 1809 and is alleged to be the oldest continuously operating store in the nation. It's a good place to buy local foods and gourmet items, baskets and pottery, fine upholstered furniture and antiques, and Christmas decorations (displayed year-round).

ACCOMMODATIONS
$50-100

Next to Hampton Inn at the airport, the **Best Western** (2138 Post Rd., Warwick, 401/737-7400 or 800/251-1962, www.bwprovidence.com, $50) has 103 units, including a few suites with wet bars and refrigerators. The property's slogan, "luxury for less," is a bit optimistic, but the rooms are pleasantly decorated as far as economy chains go, and the staff is consistently helpful and friendly.

Just three miles north of the airport are the region's two least-expensive chain properties, the **Motel 6** (20 Jefferson Blvd., Warwick, 401/467-9800 or 800/466-8356, www.motel6.com, $50-72) and the **La Quinta Inn** (36 Jefferson Blvd., Warwick, 401/941-6600 or 800/753-3757, www.lq.com, $95-119). Both are perfectly fine if you just need a cheap clean bed for the night.

One of the better and newer options, the **Courtyard Marriott Providence-Warwick** (55 Jefferson Park Rd., 401/467-6900 or 800/321-2211, www.courtyard.com, $99-179) has attractive, airy rooms and some nice perks, such as free high-speed Internet and a very good continental breakfast. It also has a pool, an exercise room, and larger rooms with whirlpool tubs or separate living areas with kitchenettes; some rooms have balconies. It's just three miles north of the airport—easy driving distance from downtown Providence.

$100-150

Best among the lower-priced properties in these parts, the **Holiday Inn Express** (901 Jefferson Blvd., Warwick, 401/736-5000 or 800/315-2621, www.hiexpress.com, $117-169) is just off the Post Road, west of the airport. There are 147 guest rooms, including 31 suites, plus full business services, an indoor pool, a small gym, and a hot tub.

The **Hilton Garden Inn** (1 Thurber St., Warwick, 401/734-9600 or 877/782-9444, www.hiltongardeninn.com, $118-139) is the newest hotel option in the Warwick area.

A couple of properties in town are better suited to longer-term guests (usually business travelers, but these can also be good choices for families

and leisure travelers). The **Residence Inn by Marriott** (500 Kilvert St., Warwick, 401/737-7100 or 800/331-3131, www.residenceinn.com, $109-209) is 0.5 miles west of the airport, just off I-95. In West Warwick, **SpringHill Suites by Marriott** (14 J. P. Murphy Hwy., 401/822-1244 or 888/287-9400, www.springhillsuites.com, $129-149) also caters to long-term stays. Each unit has separate sleeping, eating, and working areas as well as a sleeper sofa. Other amenities include in-room refrigerators, microwaves, coffeemakers, and wet bars, plus there's an on-site exercise room and indoor pool.

In Cranston, the 18-room **Edgewood Manor** (232 Norwood Ave., 401/781-0099 or 800/882-3285, www.providence-lodging.com, $129-269) is a grand early 1900s Greek Revival mansion with five beautifully crafted fireplaces and ornate architectural detailing. Guest rooms and suites carry out the building's lavish theme, with plush linens, Oriental rugs, four-poster beds, neatly framed paintings and prints, paneled walls, and high-style Victorian antiques.

$150-250

The only upscale chain property that's not directly facing the airport, the **Crowne Plaza** (801 Greenwich Ave., Warwick, 401/732-6000 or 800/227-6963, www.crowneplaza.com, $150-200) sits two miles southwest, near I-95's exit 12, on an attractively landscaped 80-acre plot. The bulk of the clientele are business travelers, who appreciate the many amenities, including free shuttle service to the airport, a popular wine bar with 24 wines served by the glass, an indoor pool and fitness center, a full business center, and a sauna and whirlpool. The facilities are in tip-top shape, the rooms large and well-equipped, and the staff friendly if not necessarily more efficient than the employees at most of the less pricey chain properties by the airport. Weekend packages are sometimes offered with certain meals are included. The restaurant presents a lavish Sunday brunch on holidays that's well attended by both guests and nonguests.

The Crowne Plaza's most obvious competitor, the 207-room **Sheraton Providence Airport** (1850 Post Rd., Warwick, 401/738-4000 or

OUTSIDE PROVIDENCE

800/325-3535, www.sheraton.com) occupies a rather dated-looking building within view of the airport and offers rates generally about 10 percent to 25 percent lower than the Crowne Plaza. Rest assured that once you're past the drab exterior you'll find a brightly furnished and well-managed contemporary property with about 200 nicely proportioned guest rooms, a restaurant, a fitness center, and an indoor pool. Sheraton has put quite a lot of money into this place in recent years, and its efforts show.

Rates at the **Hampton Inn and Suites** (2100 Post Rd., Warwick, 401/739-8888 or 800/426-7866, www.hamptoninn.com) run about the same as the others along this stretch but sometimes creep a bit higher. Considering this and the beautifully kept guest rooms and public spaces, this is an excellent choice, whether you just need a night close to the airport or a good base for visiting the entire region. Rooms are homey, with high-quality furnishings, and a fireplace warms a lobby lounge that feels comfortable for reading or relaxing, unlike many hotel lobbies. Amenities include an indoor pool, continental breakfast, a gym, a whirlpool, a business center, a game room, two-line phones, and coffeemakers.

Along the same stretch, the **Comfort Inn** (1940 Post Rd., Warwick, 401/732-0470 or 877/424-6423, www.comfortinn.com) sits right next to Bertucci's Pizza and Atwood Grill (casual American food) but has few other distinguishing features. Considering its rates are typically no lower than the Hampton Inn's, it should be considered a last choice. Nothing is especially wrong with it, but the decor, staff, and amenities are just so-so. Some rooms have whirlpool baths.

Nearly across the street from the airport entrance, the **Radisson Airport Hotel** (2081 Post Rd., Warwick, 401/739-3000 or 800/395-7046, www.radisson.com) has rates that are comparable to or sometimes even better than its competitors. It nearly adjoins Legal Seafoods and also has its own decent restaurant, and about 40 suites have whirlpool baths and wet bars. There's also a business center. It's a fairly ordinary-looking building, but the big plus is that the hotel is staffed by young and enthusiastic students from the Johnson and Wales's hospitality program, which means you can usually count on highly responsive and cheerful service as well as clean rooms.

SPORTS AND RECREATION

The **Mickey Stevens Sports Complex** (975 Sandy Lane, 401/738-2000, ext. 6800) is Warwick's recreation facility, with a public ice- and inline skating rink (401/738-2000, ext. 6810), a one-mile walking and jogging path, basketball courts, eight lighted tennis courts, three baseball diamonds, and two volleyball courts, plus a public swimming pool (401/738-2000, ext. 6809).

Beaches

Warwick has the best beaches in Greater Providence, including **Goddard Memorial State Park** (1095 Ives Rd., 401/884-2010 or 401/884-9620 in season, www.riparks.org) and 126-acre **Warwick City Park** (401/738-2000), which has a saltwater beach, changing facilities, bike paths, hiking, and ball fields. It's said, although not verified, that the very first clambake was held here in the late 1800s. Sheltered **Oakland Beach** (401/738-2000) at the southern tip of Oakland Avenue off Route 117 is a smaller swath of sand that's near several restaurants and bars; there's also a restored carousel, a big hit with kids.

Boating

Warwick is interior Rhode Island's boating capital, with more marinas, moorings, and slips than any other city in the state. Some of the larger marinas include **Apponaug Harbor Marina** (17 Arnold's Neck Dr., 401/739-5005), with 204 slips and 30 moorings; **Brewer Yacht Club** (100 Folly Landing, 401/884-0544), with 240 slips and 10 moorings; **C-Lark Marina** (252 Second Point Rd., 401/739-3871), with 350 slips; **Greenwich Bay Marina** (1 Masthead Dr., 401/884-1810), with 320 moorings; and **Norton's Shipyard** (foot of Division St., 401/884-8828), with 160 slips and 160 moorings.

Biking

The **Cranston Bike Path** offers 5.5 miles of

a beach in Warwick

pancake-flat terrain along a former railway bed. Parking is on the Cranston-Warwick border just off Pontiac Avenue (below I-295).

Golf

A windswept, fairly level course that runs fairly long, **Cranston Country Club** (69 Burlingame Rd., 401/826-1683, www.cranstoncc.com, 6 A.M.–dusk daily, $39 for 18 holes, $27 for 9 holes Mon.–Thurs., $45 for 18 holes, $27 for 9 holes Fri.–Sun.) is known for its sizable greens that demand skillful putting.

FOOD

Warwick has dozens of restaurants, many of them chains, and many of these lie along the busy Route 2 retail strip. Along here you'll find Pizzeria Uno, Red Lobster, Olive Garden, Lone Star Steakhouse, and Friday's, among many others. Warwick, Cranston, and East Greenwich are somewhat upscale suburbs, so quite a few notable chefs have opened restaurants in this area in recent years, especially in East Greenwich's quaint downtown.

Upscale

One of the better-known dining options in these parts, the **Post Office Cafe** (11 Main St., East Greenwich, 401/885-4444, www.pinellimarrarestaurants.com, 4:30–9:30 P.M. Tues.–Thurs., 4:30–10:30 P.M. Fri.–Sat., $14–24) actually occupies the town's original circa-1930 post office. It's a bright high-ceilinged space with friendly, refined service and excellent contemporary Italian fare. The same owners operate the Grille on Main, Pinelli's, and several other great Rhode Island restaurants. You might start with sautéed calamari with fire-roasted peppers and served with a champagne-garlic-butter sauce. The Post Office *frutti di mare* has a loyal following, as does the slow-simmered wild-mushroom risotto with truffle oil. There's also an impressive wine list. This place fills up fast on weekends; book well ahead.

Excellent Mediterranean and Greek fare is served at **Efendi's Mediterranean Grill** (1255 Reservoir Ave., Cranston, 401/943-8800, www.efendisbarandgrill.com, 11 A.M.–9 P.M. daily, $11–19), a laid-back restaurant with sophisticated cooking that rises above its casual environs. Specialties include rack of lamb confit with fresh-herb red wine sauce; Turkish *izgara kofte* (ground beef with spices and vegetables served with *tzatziki*); and seafood kebabs. Pita sandwiches are offered at lunch, and the Sunday brunch draws a sizable crowd for a mix of traditional breakfast fare and more savory grills and egg creations.

Arguably the best all-around dining option in the West Bay region is a meal at **Table 28** (28 Water St., East Greenwich, 401/885-1170, www.table28.com, 5:30–9 P.M. daily, $17–32), worth the drive from anywhere in the state. The kitchen takes relatively simple staples of contemporary American cuisine and presents them artfully with unusual ingredients. For instance, there's a terrific starter of crispy calamari paired with charred jalapeño-tomato sauce and roasted garlic-lemon aioli. Top main dishes include plantain-crusted fried snapper with shiitake stir-fried rice, baby bok choy, and mango chutney, and butter-basted lobster risotto with sun-dried tomatoes, *gremolata,* and crispy shallots. Save room for the signature chocolate pudding.

Creative but Casual

The **Grille on Main** (50 Main St., East Greenwich, 401/885-2200, www.pinellimarrarestaurants.com, 11:30 A.M.–10 P.M. Sun.–Tues., 11:30 A.M.–11 P.M. Wed.–Thurs., 11:30 A.M.–midnight Fri.–Sat., $8–16) is a swanky little eatery on this pretty village's dapper Main Street. Singles appreciate the long and comfy wooden bar, where you can also order from the food menu. Tables in front look out through a bow-front window over the busy sidewalk. The urbane dining room, with lavender trim and tightly spaced wooden tables, is noisy and fun. The menu changes often, and highlights include focaccia stuffed with mozzarella, vine-ripened tomatoes, fresh basil, and garlic; an excellent Buffalo chicken salad; and more substantial dishes such as oven-baked haddock topped with Ritz cracker crumbs and a citrus vinaigrette, or blackened Cajun chicken Alfredo pasta. Burgers and creative pizzas are also offered, plus lavish desserts.

The owners of the popular Chardonnay's restaurant just over the border in Seekonk, Massachusetts, operate the similarly excellent **Meritage** (5454 Post Rd., 401/884-1255, www.meritageri.com, 4:30–10 P.M. Sun.–Wed., 4:30–11 P.M. Thurs.–Sat., $12–26) in East Greenwich. This spacious, lively place is known for its eclectic menu, which offers everything from sushi to designer pizzas to creative pastas to artful grills. The pan-seared sesame tuna steak served rare with wasabi aioli is a favorite, but don't overlook the hearty pork medallions gratiné with Dijon mustard, brown sugar, and port wine, finished with Gorgonzola. Note that there's also a branch of Chardonnay's, which features the same menu, in Seekonk at 393 Taunton Ave., 508/336-0967.

The famous Boston fish house **Legal Sea Foods** (2099 Post Rd., Warwick, 401/SEA-FOOD—401/732-3663, www.legalseafoods.com, 11:30 A.M.–10 P.M. Mon.–Thurs., 11:30 A.M.–10:30 P.M. Fri., noon–9 P.M. Sat.–Sun., $11–27) has a popular branch across the street from T. F. Green Airport, and even with Rhode Island's many considerable seafood eateries, Legal draws plenty of kudos. Eat either on the casual deck, where you can watch planes taking off and landing, or in the clubby, masculine interior. Favorite starters include blackened sashimi tuna, bluefish pâté, marinated grilled calamari with white beans and grilled onions, and the restaurant's trademark clam chowder. Lobsters are the most popular entrée offering, but you'll find a large selection of grilled and fried fish platters.

A smart and contemporary space with light-wood furnishings, matte-green walls, and a couple of booths, **Culinary Affair** (650 Oaklawn Ave., Cranston, 401/944-4555, 11 A.M.–3 P.M. Mon., 11 A.M.–9 P.M. Tues.–Sat., $6–18) serves both unusual and rather expected American and Italian dishes. Grilled squid over couscous with baby greens and an orange vinaigrette makes a tempting starter. Tasty entrées include penne with grilled shrimp and plum tomatoes in a cracked pepper–Dijon sauce, or veal paillard grilled with broccoli rabe and carrot mashed potatoes.

You'll find superb, creative Italian fare at

Cafe Fresco (301 Main St., East Greenwich, 401/398-0027, www.cafefrescori.com, 5 P.M.–close daily, $12–24), a snazzy, high-ceilinged space with tall windows and banquette seating. A raw bar turns out oysters, littlenecks, and a house specialty called Oyster Fresco, topped with raspberry vinaigrette, sour cream, and caviar. Top-flight starters are bruschetta topped with shredded Black Angus beef and a creamy shallot sauce, and seared-tuna sashimi over mixed baby greens, while memorable main dishes include portobello risotto; shrimp *fra diavolo*; and clams and sausage with tomatoes, onions, and garlic over mashed potatoes.

Pizza, Pasta, and Pub Grub

In Cranston, head to **Papa Razzi** (Garden City Center, 1 Paparazzi Way, 401/942-2900, www.paparazzitrattoria.com, 11:30 A.M.–10 P.M. Mon.–Thurs., 11:30 A.M.–11 P.M. Fri.–Sat., 11:30 A.M.–9 P.M. Sun., pizzas $10–11, entrées $12–26) for pizzas and pastas. This is a classic trattoria with a couple of twists: On Monday nights opera classics are performed, and on weekends there's a fantastic brunch. Stars from the kitchen include slow-roasted lemon-garlic chicken with wilted greens and roasted potatoes, a terrific rendition of spaghetti Bolognese (with pancetta, ground veal, mushrooms, and a light tomato-cream sauce), and the pizza topped with prosciutto, mozzarella, arugula, and balsamic tomatoes.

In historic Apponaug Village, the **Remington House Inn** (3376 Post Rd., Apponaug Village, 401/736-8388, www.theremingtonhouseinn.com, 4–10 P.M. Sun.–Thurs., 4–11 P.M. Fri.–Sat., $15–18) is a charming colonial inn marred only slightly by its very busy location. Inside you'll find an inviting spot with hanging brass pots, a dark timber ceiling, and a redbrick fireplace that glows all winter long. There aren't a lot of surprises on the American-Italian menu, but portions are large and the food is well-prepared. You might sample chicken sautéed with roasted red peppers, garlic, onion, tomato, and fresh herbs tossed with bowtie pasta in a mascarpone-cream sauce; or lamb tenderloin charbroiled and finished with a merlot sauce. Clams

Remington is a worthy appetizer for the Ocean State—the tender bivalves come sautéed with Portuguese *chourico* sausage, fresh tomatoes, garlic, and onion. There are many draft beers offered, and there's an impressive wine list.

Ward's Publick House (3854 Post Rd., Warwick, 401/884-7008, www.wardspublickhouse.com, 4 P.M.–close daily, $8–12) fits the bill if you're craving decent pub fare and a pint of imported draught beer (Harp, Guinness, Tetley's, Speckled Hen, and Murphy's are all on tap). For sustenance, try the stir-fried veggies, traditional Irish bangers and mash, shepherd's pie, or blackened salmon. There's traditional Irish music many evenings. Whether for a meal or for drinks, this is a festive and atmospheric hangout with warm pub decor.

In East Greenwich, yuppies and yachting types flock to **20 Water Street** (20 Water St., East Greenwich, 401/885-3703, www.twentywaterstreet.com, 11:30 A.M.–close daily, $15–23 in the dining room, $9–15 in the tavern and on deck), a festive waterside bar and eatery with a lovely deck overlooking the many sailboats and fishing trawlers on Narragansett Bay—it looks out toward Goddard Park. The dining room, decked with hardwood floors, Windsor chairs, and dark-wood paneled walls, presents a somewhat upscale menu of seafood favorites, such as clams casino, seafood casserole with a sherry-wine lemon butter, and rack of lamb with garlic and rosemary. More casual fare is served on the deck and in the tavern, including grilled swordfish steak, lobster rolls, and Caesar salad. By most accounts, the tavern fare is both better tasting and a better value.

Chelo's Waterfront Bar and Grille (2225 Post Rd., Warwick, 401/737-7299, www.chelos.com, 11:30 A.M.–10:30 P.M. Mon.–Thurs., 11:30 A.M.–11:30 P.M. Fri.–Sat., noon–10 P.M. Sun., $7–15) overlooks the bay and serves casual seafood and American fare.

Ethnic Fare

Providence takes the prize in Rhode Island when it comes to ethnic fine cuisine, but the burbs have caught up fast in recent years. Take the **Cucina Mista** (455 S. Main St., East Greenwich,

OUTSIDE PROVIDENCE

401/398-2900, www.cucinamista.com dinner daily, year-round, $10–18), which serves commendable pastas and creative salads, grilled meats, and a remarkably flavorful risotto.

You can get your sushi fix at **Haruki** (1210 Oaklawn Ave., Cranston, 401/463-8338, www.harukisushi.com, lunch 11:30 A.M.– 2:30 P.M. Mon.–Fri., noon–3 P.M. Sat., dinner 5–9:30 P.M. Mon.–Thurs., 5–10 P.M. Fri.–Sat., 4:30–9:30 P.M. Sun., $9–17); you'll seldom dine alone at this phenomenally popular spot on busy Oaklawn Avenue inside a bright, beautiful dining room with varnished wood trim and elegant Japanese murals. There's an extensive and reasonably priced sushi menu—unusual options include the yellowtail and scallion rolls, sea urchin, and spicy codfish roe. Specialties from the grill vary from crispy fried catfish with wasabi and light pepper-onion sauce to scallops teriyaki and honey-barbecued pork ribs.

Quick Bites

Iggy's Doughboys (889 Oakland Beach Ave., Warwick, 401/737-9459, www.iggysdoughboys. com, 11 A.M.–10 P.M. Sun.–Thurs., 11 A.M.– 11 P.M. Fri.–Sun. summer, 11 A.M.–7 P.M. Sun.–Thurs., 11 A.M.–8 P.M. Fri.–Sat. winter, $3–9) might just serve the best clam cakes in the state—it's certainly fun to test them out against the many reputable competitors around Rhode Island. The original Iggy's opened in 1924 and has withstood hurricanes and recessions; the view, out toward Newport Bridge, Jamestown, and across to the East Bay, is outstanding— you'll actually feel as though you're down by the ocean. Standard fare includes chowder, stuffies, fried scallops, the famous Iggy Burger with sautéed peppers and onions, tuna grinders, meatball subs, and chicken wings. Iggy's also specializes in greasy little fried doughboys, which are dusted liberally with powdered sugar; a half dozen costs just $2.95. The website has coupons discounting several items on the menu.

You'll find a nice selection of tasty sub sandwiches at **Carmine's Sub Shop** (310 Atwood Ave., Cranston, 401/942-9600, 9 A.M.–7 P.M. daily, under $5). Fillings include veal steak, meatballs, and a wide and tempting array

of cold cuts. Pick up a couple (or a few...or a plateful) of New York wieners at **Peter's Coney Island System** (2298 West Shore Rd., Warwick, 401/732-6499, under $4), one of the legions of exceptional purveyors of these addictive treats scattered around the state.

A meager burger stand when Jigger Lindberg opened it in 1918, **Jigger's Diner** (145 Main St., East Greenwich, 401/884-5388, 6 A.M.–2 P.M. Mon.–Fri., 6 A.M.–1 P.M. Sat.– Sun., $5–11) serves some of Rhode Island's best diner fare, from the trademark gingerbread pancakes to more prosaic dishes such as eggs and bacon. This may not be fancy food, but it's definitely not your typical greasy-spoon cooking either—presentation verges on elaborate, with fresh and inventive ingredients, such as the sandwich of fresh mozzarella, pesto, and vine-ripened tomatoes; or pan-roasted cod topped with salsa fresca (a dinner entrée served Fridays only, when the restaurant also allows patrons to bring their own wine or beer). The fries are hand-cut and homemade, as is the breakfast sausage. It's one of the oldest restaurants in town and is housed in a little railroad car with a blue facade along the ranks of pretty shops in East Greenwich.

Head to **Sweet Temptations** (450 Main St., East Greenwich, 401/884-2404) for freshly made cakes and sweets as well as deli sandwiches and light breakfast fare that use the bakery's exceptional fresh breads. **Dear Hearts** (2214 Broad St., Cranston, 401/272-2000, ext. 1, www.dearhearts.com, 10 A.M.–10 P.M. daily) doles out about 50 varieties of delicious homemade ice cream.

Java Joints

Grab a light lunch, pastries and baked goods, or a cup of espresso at **SimonSays Cafe** (96 Main St., 401/884-1965, 6:30 A.M.–6 P.M. daily), a fun little coffeehouse in downtown East Greenwich.

Gourmet Goods and Picnic Supplies

Home of the intriguing and strangely satisfying stuffed pickle, **Pickles Gourmet Deli** (135

Frenchtown Rd., East Greenwich, 401/884-1828, www.picklescustomcatering.com, 9 A.M.–3 P.M. Mon.–Sat., $3–8) also serves about 30 kinds of breakfast and lunch sandwiches, plus homemade quiche and stuffed eggplant tortes.

Rhode Island Monthly magazine once had a bunch of second-grade schoolkids in Barrington taste-test cookies from a few of the state's most reputable bakeries. **Rainbow Bakery** (800 Reservoir Ave., Cranston, 401/944-8180, www.rainbowbakeryri.com, 7 A.M.–5 P.M. Tues.–Fri., 7 A.M.–2 P.M. Sat., 7 A.M.–1 P.M. Sun.) took the prize for the best chocolate-chip cookies; it's hard to argue with such a reputable panel of experts.

VISITOR INFORMATION

Pamphlets, brochures, and visitor information are available from the **Providence Warwick Convention and Visitors Bureau** (144 Westminster St., 401/456-0200, www.goprovidence.com). You can also get information on the Warwick and Cranston area from the **Warwick Tourism Office** (Warwick City Hall, 3275 Post Rd., 401/738-2000, ext. 6402, www.visitwarwickri.com).

OUTSIDE PROVIDENCE

Points West

The largely rural and sparsely populated towns of western Rhode Island, like those just across the border in eastern Connecticut, have relatively few attractions and notable sights. You will find a handful of enchanting small villages characterized mostly by rolling woodland, obsolete but often handsome mills, and fast-growing tracts of suburban housing. There are very few accommodations in these parts, and extremely limited public transportation. But it is an ideal region for relaxing country drives, bike rides, or moderately hilly strolls.

GLOCESTER

One of the state's largest towns, Glocester comprises about 56 square miles, even more than its large neighbor to the north, Burrillville. It was once part of Providence, which occupied most of northern Rhode Island until the 1730s. Coal mining, potash making, iron forging, marble quarrying, felt-hat making, and cottonseed oil manufacture were among the eclectic industries this town supported, along with farming, which remains to a small extent today. The town has just under 10,000 residents, making the population density among the lowest in the state.

CHEPACHET

From Providence, U.S. 44 cuts west up through Glocester and into its most notable village, Chepachet, which lies at the crossing of Routes 100/102 and U.S. 44. This pretty village embodies the sleepy pace of northwestern Rhode Island while also defying the stereotype that there's little to see or do in these parts. Main

COURTESY OF BLACKSTONE VALLEY TOURISM COUNCIL

Cherry Valley Herb Farm in Glocester

Street abounds with antiques and other unusual shops, and you can get a brief lesson in state history by visiting the bronze plaque marking the site of the 1842 Dorr Rebellion, an event that threw Rhode Island politics into chaos.

In Chepachet you can also visit the **Job Armstrong Store** (1181 Main St., U.S. 44, 401/568-8967, www.glocesterheritagesociety. org, 11 A.M.–2 P.M. Thurs. and Sat. Apr.–Dec., by appointment only Jan.–Mar., free), which was the largest of 13 dry-goods stores in this village in the early 1800s. Today it has been converted into a living-history museum, where you can watch crafts, spinning, quilting, and rug-hooking demonstrations. It's also the headquarters of the Glocester Heritage Society and a visitors center with information on the area's few local attractions.

Just south of Chepachet you'll find **Sprague Farm** (Pine Orchard Rd., 401/588-9124, www. glocesterlandtrust.org), a 291-acre site administered by the Glocester Land Trust and containing mature evergreens, striped maples, and Atlantic white cedars. There are also flower gardens and shrubs as well as several stone bridges of note.

SCITUATE AND FOSTER

From Providence, U.S. 6 eventually leads west into Scituate and then on to the Connecticut border via Foster. It's a fairly nondescript drive through these parts aside from a stop in the town's administrative center, North Scituate, an endearingly unfussy village of mostly white clapboard colonial houses. North Scituate is entirely ingenious—unsullied by development and still totally free of banal attempts at gentrification. There's nothing cutesy here, just a few historic buildings that always seem to need a fresh coat of paint.

One of Scituate's best-known features is six-mile-long Scituate Reservoir, a narrow waterway that terminates at the immense 3,200-foot-long Scituate Dam. The state created the reservoir in the 1920s by relocating about 1,600 residents of seven villages— Kent, South Scituate, Ashland, Richmond, Rockland, Saundersville, and Ponganset—and

flooding the entire basin. It's now the state's largest body of fresh water and provides water for about two of every three Rhode Island households. You can drive around parts of the 60-mile shoreline, but recreational activity— including fishing, boating, and hiking—is strictly forbidden.

Still farther west, Little Foster Center is the civic hub of the large but sparsely populated town of Foster. By Rhode Island standards it's quite hilly and rugged, its slopes feeding into the Moosup and Ponaganset Rivers. Anchoring this village is the **Foster Town House** (180 Howard Hill Rd., 401/392-9200, www.townoffoster. com, 8:30 A.M.–5:30 P.M. Mon.–Thurs., free). This 1796 two-story building was built and used as a Baptist church until the 1840s.

COVENTRY

You can follow Route 117 from the busy suburbs of Cranston and West Warwick to the quiet township of Coventry, at 62 square miles the second-largest town in the state. The village of Washington, the civic seat, was the site of mills specializing in lace, cotton, and wool during the 19th century.

In the Anthony section of town, just north of Washington, lived the famous colonial military statesman Nathanael Greene. Born to Quaker parents in 1752, the distinguished general lived in the **Nathanael Greene Homestead** (50 Taft St., 401/821-8630, 10 A.M.–5 P.M. Wed. and Sat., 1–5 P.M. Sun. Apr.–Oct., or by appointment, $5 adults, $2 children) from 1770 to 1776, after which it was owned by his brother, Jacob. The 2.5-story frame house has two chimneys and sits on a bluff by the south branch of the Pawtuxet River. Every room in the house contains a paneled fireplace and three double-hung windows; it has been a museum since it was restored in 1924 and contains furnishings and artifacts from the Greene family. It's believed that the cannon in front of the house was made at the Greene family forge in Potowomut.

SHOPPING

In a cavernous vintage red barn in Glocester, **Cherry Valley Herb Farm** (969 Snake Hill Rd., Glocester, 401/568-8585, www.cherryvalleyherbfarm.com, by appointment only) sells a wide array of mostly country French collectibles, home furnishings, and garden accoutrements, plus gourmet jams and sauces and a long list of herbs and spices. Another nearby spot with both a year-round Christmas Shop and a wide array of toys, teddy bears, dolls, and gifts is **Johnson's Farm and Santa's Workshop** (33 Money Hill Rd., Glocester, 401/568-1693, 10 A.M.–6 P.M. Mon.–Fri., 10 A.M.–5 P.M. Sat.).

John and Cindy's Harvest Acres Farms (425 Kingstown Rd., South Kingstown, 401/789-8752, 10 A.M.–6 P.M. daily) is an extensive farmstead with fresh honey, maple syrup, sweet corn, tomatoes, mums, milk, eggs, fresh fruit and jams, and pumpkins. Pick fresh fruit, fall pumpkins and Indian corn, and other seasonal goods at **The Junction** (1194 Putnam Pike, Chepachet, 401/568-4619). Here you can also browse the extensive selection of garden statuary, candles, antique furnishings, plants, and flowers. Beginning in June, fresh strawberries, raspberries, sweet corn, pumpkins, and hay are the order of the day all summer long at **Salisbury Farm** (Rte. 14 at Plainfield Pike and Pippin Orchard Rd., Johnston, 401/942-9741, www.salisburyfarm. com, 7 A.M.–6 P.M. Fri.–Wed., 7 A.M.–8 P.M. Thurs.), which was founded in the 1800s and has been run by five generations of the Salisbury family. The farm also contains an intricate corn maze, the first of its kind in New England. About a mile of pathways cuts through four acres of corn rows—it's no easy feat finding your way out. In the fall, you can go on hayrides.

SPORTS AND RECREATION

In the towns west of Providence, beyond the immediate suburbs, you'll find copious opportunities for hiking, biking, fishing, and enjoying the outdoors. West of Warwick is the **Arcadia Management Area,** a 14,000-acre preserve that passes through Richmond, Hopkinton, and Exeter. It has two freshwater beaches along Beach Road (off Rte. 165) and also one at Browning Mill Pond (off Arcadia Rd.). You can pursue hunting, fishing, hiking, mountain biking, and horseback riding in the preserve.

Hiking

A half-hour drive west of Providence, an excellent spot for a ramble is Exeter's **Beach Pond,** which lies half in Rhode Island's Beach Pond State Forest and half in Voluntown, Connecticut's Pachaug State Forest (access is off Rte. 165, about 6 miles west of Rte. 3). From the parking area, head to marked trails of varying lengths that climb through hemlock and birch forest, around the north shore of the pond, and through some quite steep valleys. An additional network of trails meanders south of the pond, nearly as far as Route 138. These blazed trails cross several scenic stream beds and wooded glens. The pond is also a popular spot for fishing and boating. This is one of several popular hiking areas off Route 165, which cuts through some of the state's prettiest and least populated terrain. Other hikes to consider are the Mt. Tom, Bald Hill, and Stepstone Falls trails.

ACCOMMODATIONS
$50-100

Best Western West Greenwich Inn (101 Nooseneck Hill Rd., West Greenwich, 401/397-5494 or 800/528-1234, www.bestwestern.com, $69–99) is one of the best lodging options in these parts. The 56-room hotel tends to have rates comparable to the less desirable nearby Super 8. It's on attractive wooded grounds but has no restaurant.

$100-150

There's a top-notch **Hampton Inn** (850 Centre of New England Blvd., Coventry, 401/823-4041 or 800/426-7866, www.hamptoninn. com, $100–139) in Coventry, just off I-95 exit 7, close to West Warwick and East Greenwich. It has all the usual perks of Hampton Inns, including a nice fitness center, pool, and hot tub, and some king studio suites, which have kitchenettes, living rooms, and whirlpool tubs.

FOOD
Creative but Casual

A relative newcomer in inviting Harmony, **Chester's** (102 Putnam Pike, U.S. 44, 401/949-1846, Harmony, 11 A.M.–1 A.M. daily, $7–13) doles out respectable portions of comfort foods, many of the dishes with nouvelle tendencies, including veal saltimbocca, chicken sautéed with sun-dried tomatoes, mushrooms, and pasta with a pink cream sauce, and scallops Nantucket baked with bacon and cheddar. Burgers are a big hit, as is the fried calamari. A fieldstone fireplace warms the dining room.

Pizza, Pasta, and Pub Grub

Gentlemen Farmer Restaurant (845 Providence St., West Warwick, 401/615-7777, www.genltemenfarmerrestaurant.com, 6 A.M.–8 P.M. daily, $3–11) is a delightful little stone-and-timber pizzeria and diner where locals hang out and the waitresses call you "hon." There's a long and varied menu, and portions are huge and well-priced, with about 20 kinds of grinder, a variety of pizzas, seafood platters, bacon burgers, hot dogs, Greek salads, barbecued pork sandwiches, and hearty breakfast fare. Most of this stuff will give your arteries a good hardening, but it's tasty cooking.

The **Tavern on Main** (1157 Putnam Pike, Chepachet, 401/710-9788, www.tavernonmainri.com, 4–9 P.M. Wed.–Thurs., 11:30 A.M.–9:30 P.M. Fri.–Sat., 11:30 A.M.–8:30 P.M. Sun., $11–22) serves mostly traditional American dishes (prime rib, steak, seafood casseroles, and pizzas) plus some kicky ethnic takes such as teriyaki-marinated steak tips and chicken marsala. Ask the friendly staff about the tavern ghost, and you'll get an earful about alleged sightings; they host ghost dinners on Wednesday nights.

Quick Bites

You can't miss **Cindy's Diner** (46 Hartford Ave., North Scituate, 401/934-2449, 6 A.M.–8 P.M. Sat.–Thurs., 6 A.M.–9 P.M. Fri., under $8) with its glittering pink, blue, and yellow neon sign. It's a big hit with the breakfast crowd. **Shady Acres Restaurant and Dairy Bar** (164 Danielson Pike, Foster, 401/647-7019, 6 A.M.–8 P.M. daily, under $6) is a typical roadside short-order eatery with a long menu of delicious home-baked pies and ice creams. Burgers and fried seafood are also offered, and breakfast is served early. If you find yourself hungry out near Arcadia Management Area, there's always the **Middle of Nowhere Diner** (222 Nooseneck Hill Rd., U.S. 3, Exeter, 401/397-8855, 5 A.M.–8:30 P.M. daily, under $6), a simple clapboard eatery with tasty short-order cooking, including fantastic omelets.

www.moon.com

DESTINATIONS | ACTIVITIES | BLOGS | MAPS | BOOKS

MOON.COM is ready to help plan your next trip! Filled with fresh trip ideas and strategies, author interviews, informative travel blogs, a detailed map library, and descriptions of all the Moon guidebooks, Moon.com is all you need to get out and explore the world—or even places in your own backyard. While at Moon.com, sign up for our monthly e-newsletter for updates on new releases, travel tips, and expert advice from our on-the-go Moon authors. As always, when you travel with Moon, expect an experience that is uncommon and truly unique.

MOON IS ON FACEBOOK—BECOME A FAN!
JOIN THE MOON PHOTO GROUP ON FLICKR

MAP SYMBOLS

··········	Expressway	◖	Highlight	✗	Airfield	⚲	Golf Course
········	Primary Road	○	City/Town	✈	Airport	**P**	Parking Area
	Secondary Road	◉	State Capital	▲	Mountain	⬛	Archaeological Site
· · · · ·	Unpaved Road	⊛	National Capital	✦	Unique Natural Feature	⚱	Church
- - - - -	Trail	★	Point of Interest			⬛	Gas Station
············	Ferry	•	Accommodation	🦢	Waterfall	〰	Glacier
- - - - -	Railroad	▼	Restaurant/Bar	▲	Park		Mangrove
	Pedestrian Walkway	▪	Other Location	⬛	Trailhead		Reef
)))))))))	Stairs	▲	Campground	⛷	Skiing Area		Swamp

CONVERSION TABLES

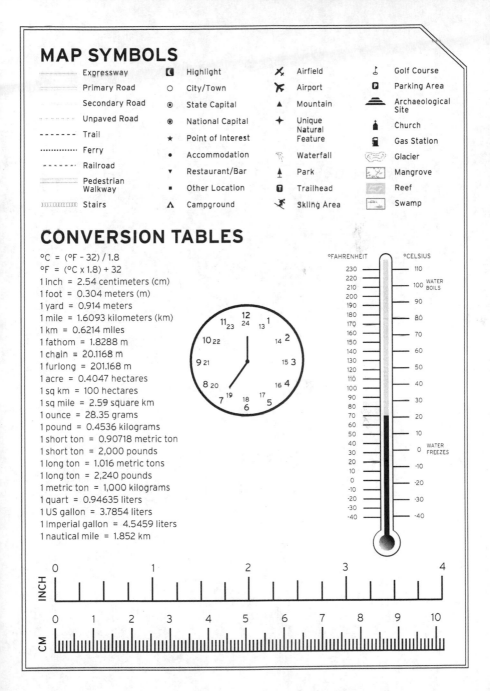

°C = (°F - 32) / 1.8
°F = (°C x 1.8) + 32
1 inch = 2.54 centimeters (cm)
1 foot = 0.304 meters (m)
1 yard = 0.914 meters
1 mile = 1.6093 kilometers (km)
1 km = 0.6214 miles
1 fathom = 1.8288 m
1 chain = 20.1168 m
1 furlong = 201.168 m
1 acre = 0.4047 hectares
1 sq km = 100 hectares
1 sq mile = 2.59 square km
1 ounce = 28.35 grams
1 pound = 0.4536 kilograms
1 short ton = 0.90718 metric ton
1 short ton = 2,000 pounds
1 long ton = 1.016 metric tons
1 long ton = 2,240 pounds
1 metric ton = 1,000 kilograms
1 quart = 0.94635 liters
1 US gallon = 3.7854 liters
1 Imperial gallon = 4.5459 liters
1 nautical mile = 1.852 km

MOON SPOTLIGHT PROVIDENCE

Avalon Travel
a member of the Perseus Books Group
1700 Fourth Street   •
Berkeley, CA 94710, USA
www.moon.com

Editors: Elizabeth Hansen, Leah Gordon
Series Manager: Kathryn Ettinger
Copy Editor: Christopher Church
Graphics Coordinator: Tabitha Lahr
Production Coordinator: Tabitha Lahr
Cover Designer: Tabitha Lahr
Map Editor: Albert Angulo
Cartographers: Kat Bennett, Chris Henrick

ISBN-13: 978-1-59880-829-2

Text © 2011 by Michael Blanding and Alexandra Hall
and Avalon Travel.
Maps © 2011 by Avalon Travel.
All rights reserved.

Printed in the United States

OUTSIDE PROVIDENCE

ABOUT THE AUTHORS

Michael Blanding and Alexandra Hall

Michael Blanding and Alexandra Hall met working five feet from each other as editors at *Boston Magazine*, where Alex covered food and fashion, and Michael wrote about politics and crime. Since then, they've traveled the world together, dodging bicycles on the streets of Ho Chi Minh City, breaking an axle on a safari in South Africa, and closing out nightclubs in Reykjavik, Paris, and Buenos Aires (not an easy feat!). But wherever their travels have taken them, they've always loved returning to New England for its mix of natural beauty and culture.

Alex grew up on Boston's South Shore and studied at Wheaton College and Le Cordon Bleu in Paris. After several years as a senior editor for DailyCandy and editor for Fashion Boston, she is now back at *Boston Magazine* as executive editor for lifestyle. Michael grew up west of Boston, attended Williams College, and was a staff writer and editor at *Boston Magazine* for five years. Now a freelance magazine writer, he has also taught journalism at Emerson College, Northeastern University, and Tufts University. His first book of investigative nonfiction, *The Coke Machine: The Dirty Truth Behind the World's Favorite Soft Drink*, was recently published.

Together, Alex and Michael have written for publications including *Condé Nast Traveler, Bon Appétit, Town & Country Travel, New England Travel, Yankee, Boston Magazine, Elle Decor, Continental, Business Traveler, The Nation, The New Republic, The New York Times, The Boston Globe,* and AlterNet. They were married on the rustic shores of Maine's Moosehead Lake, where Michael wore a kilt and Alex donned red heels and white feathers. They now live in Boston's Jamaica Plain neighborhood with their cat, Catsby, and their six-year-old son Zachary and four-year-old daughter Cleo, who have fast become two of the best-traveled kids in the world.